Student Book

Partners in Learning

a family confirmation approach

Contributors:

**Jeffrey Kunze, Gregory Sawyer,
Wayne Schroeder, Roger Sonnenberg,
Timothy Wesemann**

Consultant: Dr. John Oberdeck

Edited by Edward Engelbrecht and Rodney Rathmann

Copyright © 2001 Concordia Publishing House
3558 S. Jefferson Avenue, St. Louis, MO 63118-3968
Manufactured in the United States of America

1   2   3   4   5   6   7   8   9   10   10   09   08   07   06   05   04   03   02   01

Contents

Confirmation Means Memories: Family in Faith Journal

As you and your parent or mentor read God's Word and pray together, something marvelous happens: you grow in maturity as a believer. The Family in Faith Journal provides an opportunity for you to capture that experience and create a lifelong keepsake.

Take turns with your parent or mentor writing in the journal. During the week feel free to write down your thoughts and prayers, add photographs, or even doodle. Since confirmation is such a special learning experience, your family may wish to purchase a quality journal or use a sturdy composition notebook for your writing.

See It, Say It, Hear It: Memory Work Made Easier

Almost every congregation requires memory work as part of confirmation studies. Before you panic, learn a little bit about how to do memory work so that you will be better prepared for your assignments.

When you study your memory work, you want to focus on the text in every way possible. Here are some practical steps:

1. Choose a quiet place with few distractions (no TV, radio, or computer).

2. Carefully read your memory passage out loud up to seven times in a row. (This sounds like it will take forever. But even long passages will take only about three minutes.) As you read, listen to yourself speak.

3. Close your catechism and see how much you can say out loud without mistakes.

4. When you can say the passage without opening your catechism, find someone who will listen to you recite the passage and correct your mistakes.

5. Choose a regular time of day when you can study (e.g., before or after a meal, after you get home from school).

6. Talk with your parents about making the catechism the basis of your family devotions.

If your congregation requires lots of memory work, ask for opportunities to recite passages both on the day of your confirmation classes and on Sunday morning before or after church.

Before You Are Confirmed

Lutheran churches have traditionally based confirmation on three Bible passages. Review these passages and prayerfully consider your maturity in the faith.

Matthew 28:19–20
- I am baptized in the name of the triune God.
- I have learned God's Word as summarized by the Ten Commandments, the Apostles' Creed, and the Lord's Prayer.
- I believe these teachings by the grace of God's Holy Spirit, and by His power I strive to obey them.

Matthew 10:32–33
- I publicly confess that Jesus Christ has saved me from sin by His death and resurrection.
- I actively participate in Divine Services.
- I can witness about salvation in Christ to those outside the church.

1 Corinthians 11:28
- I examine my life and faith before coming to the Lord's Supper.

Remember, confirmation is only the beginning of your life as a mature Christian. The Lord wants you to continue in worship, devotions, and Bible study throughout your life.

First Commandment

Table Talk

Did St. Francis have to give up his family's business in order to keep the First Commandment? As a cloth merchant, how might he have used his family's business to fear, love, and trust in God?

Would anyone like to share an example of something or someone that might interfere with your relationship with God?

How might keeping the First Commandment change your relationship with your family, friends, and others?

Bible Study

God defeats the Egyptians and frees the children of Israel from slavery. Through Moses, God leads the Israelites to Mount Sinai. Read Exodus 19:17–20:3.

1. What fearful things did Moses and the people of Israel experience when God drew near to Mount Sinai?

Eyes saw: _____

Ears heard: _____

Nose smelled: _____

Body felt: _____

2. Before commanding the Israelites to "have no other gods," how did the Lord remind them of His love? See Exodus 20:2.

3. Imagine that you stand at the foot of Mount Sinai, seeing and hearing the fearful things you described in question 1. What words in this story would lead you to trust God above all things?

4. Read Luke 23:39–43. Contrast what happened at Mount Sinai with what happened with God's Son, Jesus, at Mount Calvary. Why could the thief trust Jesus? See also Luke 23:34.

5. Why did God give us the Law?

6. The Law cannot save us. We cannot keep God's Law perfectly. But who has kept the Law perfectly for us and our salvation?

7. How are we Christians able to fear, love, and trust in God above all things?

Family in Faith Journal

Brainstorm with your parent or mentor three ways to keep God number one in your life. Record this in your Family in Faith Journal.

Fun for Review

Characters: Announcer, three "Team Shellfish" members (TS1, TS2, TS3), three "Team One.com" members (TOC1, TOC2, TOC3)

Setting: ANNOUNCER stands in the front of class. TEAM SHELLFISH is on one side, TEAM ONE.COM on the other.

ANNOUNCER: Ladies and gentlemen, welcome to tonight's main event. Let's get ready to ruum-mmmble! Now give it up for our first group, "Team Shellfish"!

(Players enter to applause.)

TS: *(Chanting together)* We're number one! We're number one! We're number one!

ANNOUNCER: *(To TS1)* It looks like your team is ready and pumped.

TS1: We're the best! We're number one! We're rockin' tonight and every night.

TS2: We have the biggest muscles, the fastest legs, the strongest arms . . .

TS3: We have the quickest reactions and make the fastest decisions. Without a doubt, we're number one.

TS: *(Chanting together)* We're number one! We're number one! We're number one!

ANNOUNCER: Let's meet the other group now, "Team One-dot-Com"!

(Players enter to applause.)

TOC: *(Chanting together)* You're number one! You're number one!

TS1: What are you fools saying?

TOC1: You're number one! You're number one!

TS3: What are you talking about? You're supposed to say, "We're number one!" not "You're number one!"

TOC1: But I'm not number one.

TS2: What has happened to your sense of self-esteem?

TS1: You're supposed to watch out for numero uno!

TS3: What pushovers! They're even admitting that we're number one.

TOC2: We're not saying that **you're** number one.

TS2: We're not deaf and dumb. You just said, "You're number one!" You are saying that we're number one.

TOC3: No, no, no! We're talking about the meaning of our team's name. The name of our team and our cheer remind us of what is really important—no matter what we are doing.

TOC2: One-dot-com. First Commandment. God is above all things. Get it?

TS1: Who cares? Your team is lame.

TOC1: When we say, "You're number one," we're talking to God. He's number one; we're not.

TOC3: We know that we wouldn't be able to compete tonight without Him.

TOC2: We wouldn't have legs or arms, brains or skills, eyes or ears, time or effort without Him. He's number one.

TOC3: That helps put things in the proper perspective. He's number one in everything.

TOC1: It helps us from becoming shellfish, I mean, selfish.

TOC2: And what's really great is that no matter what happens when we use our body, mind, or talents, we know the victory is ours because . . . *(pointing upwards)* You're number one! You're number one!

TS1: I hate to admit it, but they have a great point. I say let's go for the victory. And since we can't beat 'em, let's join 'em.

ALL: *(Chanting together, pointing and looking upwards)* You're number one! You're number one! You're number one!

Second and Third Commandments

Bible Study

When Moses is 80 years old, God calls him to lead the Israelites out of Egypt. In fear, Moses refuses to accept God's calling. But in response to each of Moses' objections, God gives His promises and His name. Read Exodus 3:1–15.

1. List Moses' objections in 3:11–14 and God's promises for each objection:

A. _____

_____

B. _____

_____

2. What name does God use for Himself? See verse 14.

3. Our names distinguish us from other people. How does this special name for God distinguish Him from everyone else?

4. What comfort is there in knowing that God is "I AM"?

5. How should we reverence God's name that has such meaning for us?

6. Moses did go and do what God had commanded and was blessed in his efforts. What blessings do we receive as we respond to God's command to worship each week?

7. Ask your parent/mentor to explain why he/she appreciates worship.

8. The Law cannot save us. We cannot keep God's Law perfectly. But who has kept God's Law for us and our salvation?

Family in Faith Journal

Ask your parent or mentor to briefly describe an example of giving a name to a child. Record these memories in the Family in Faith Journal. If possible, look up the meaning of your own name, and record this as well.

Fun for Review

Characters: Narrator, Suzy, Amy, Bill, Bobby

Setting: Outside church after worship

NARRATOR: Okay, here's the scene: our wonderful group of eighth graders decides to worship together. What you're about to witness could happen on any given Sunday.

(Kids enter exchanging excited comments.)

GROUP: Wow! Cool! Yeah, that was great!

SUZY: What a cool sermon! *(High fives are exchanged.)* I can't wait to go back! Yeah!

NARRATOR: *(Frantic)* WAIT! Let's be a little more realistic, shall we? You're in eighth grade, remember?

(Kids back up, go in reverse, and once again enter—a little more solemn.)

AMY: *(Proper)* That was a nice sermon.

SUZY: *(Replying to AMY, but side-glance to NARRATOR)* Yeah. I still think it was *(pause for emphasis; more politely)* rather cool.

NARRATOR: Now Bill has something to share …

BILL: Hey! Did you guys hear about my aunt?

BOBBY: Is this another bug joke?

BILL: Um … no. No joke. She's very ill. My mom says she may not make it out of the hospital.

SUZY: No way!

AMY: Wow. Sorry, Bill.

SUZY: Yeah. Sorry, man.

BILL: Thanks. I wish I would have remembered to tell the pastor so we could have prayed for her in church. Now I guess I'll have to wait until next week.

BOBBY: Why don't you pray for her tonight … or, um … now?

BILL: I don't think my prayers will really count unless they're in church. Besides, I'm not really sure how I should pray for her. Aw, just forget it. Let's go.

AMY: That's ridiculous.

SUZY: Yeah. Out of touch.

BOBBY: You can call on the name of the Lord …

AMY: … anytime!

SUZY: … anywhere!

BOBBY: Don't you remember what the pastor said? "Call upon Me when there's trouble." You don't have to wait until Sunday. You can call on the Lord for help …

AMY: … anytime!

SUZY: … anywhere!

BOBBY: Even now I know God hears your prayers. And I know He likes it when we use His name not only on Sundays but …

(AMY and SUZY are both giggling.)

AMY: … anytime!

SUZY: … anywhere!

(They high five.)

BILL: Okay! I get the picture. I just hope He hears me and understands.

BOBBY: Yes. He hears you because we pray in the name of Jesus.

AMY: And He certainly understands.

SUZY: And He's, like, way in touch with what you need, man!

BOBBY: And remember, there's no other name you ever need to call upon in trouble or praise, but the name of our triune God.

NARRATOR: And so the kids continued on their way. Bill was comforted by the fact that he can call on the name of the Lord …

ALL STUDENTS: … anytime and anywhere!

Fourth Commandment 3

Table Talk

Contrast your life today with Adrian's. Why is your life so different?

What might you tell a friend who is angry at his or her parents and thinking of running away from home?

For the Fourth Commandment, who does Luther include in his definition of those in authority?

Bible Study

Eli fails to raise his two sons in the way that they should go, and as a result both die prematurely. In contrast, Samuel heeds God's words and receives His blessings. Read 1 Samuel 2:12–36.

1. In what ways did Eli stretch God's patience too far in his service to God in the temple? See 1 Samuel 2:27–29.

2. Because Eli honored his wayward sons more than he honored God, there were some dire consequences. What were some of those consequences according to 1 Samuel 2:30–33? Read also 1 Samuel 4:10–11.

3. Consider the promise in 1 Samuel 2:35. This promise could not refer to Samuel. Its ultimate fulfillment was in someone far greater. Who was He? For help, see Hebrews 5:6.

4. Philippians 2:6–11 describes Jesus' obedience. What does His obedience on the cross mean to you and your family?

5. Name some consequences you've seen for children who have failed to "honor their parents."

6. Because of Jesus' "obedience to death" on the cross, what is the Good News for us as we consider our disobedience to Him and to our parents?

7. Read Ephesians 6:1–3. What promise does God attach to the Fourth Commandment?

Family in Faith Journal

Describe a time when your parent or mentor gave you extra special help out of love (e.g., with homework, learning a sport). Your parent or mentor should briefly describe the enormity of God's love in Jesus and record these words in the Family in Faith Journal.

Fun for Review

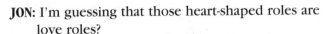

Characters: Mom, Pops, Jon, Sue. Mom and Pops have Italian accents.

Setting: Bakery

MOM: Welcome to the famous Mom and Pop's Bakery.

JON: Thanks. My sister and I heard that you have the best rolls in town.

POPS: We specialize in parental "roles."

SUE: Excuse me? Did you say, "parental roles"?

POPS: I did.

SUE: Oh … maybe we came to the wrong place.

JON: Wait a minute, Sue. Let's see what they have.

MOM: Over in this case we have some great roles filled with respect.

POPS: Everyone in the family needs those.

SUE: That sounds good, but I don't know if they would go over in my house today.

MOM: Oh, but respect roles make everything else taste good.

POPS: It's impossible to yell and fight while you're chewing a respect role.

SUE: That's cool. *(Pointing)* What are those?

POPS: Those are our teen packs of obedience-filled roles.

JON: Aren't those hard to swallow?

MOM: Contrary to popular belief, they aren't at all.

POPS: Too many people don't even try them because they don't sound good.

SUE: They wouldn't be my first choice, but I hear they're good for you.

MOM: Sometimes people don't want things that are good for them! *(Looks at POPS. Both shake heads and say, "Agh!")*

JON: I'm guessing that those heart-shaped roles are love roles?

MOM: You'll never outgrow the taste for those. Growing teenagers need them most.

POPS: That's for sure, Mama! Love never fails!

SUE: What about nutrients? Are all these roles healthful?

MOM: They make for the healthiest of relationships.

POPS: So many people hang out on the corner where they are swallowing angry, hateful, hurtful roles that can make people deadly sick. What they need are some good parental roles for a change!

JON: *(Pointing)* And this one over here looks like the best place to start—the forgiven role.

SUE: That's a great place to start. Wrap some forgiven roles to go.

JON: And box up some of those grace roles, please.

MOM: *(Boxing them up)* What else can we get you?

SUE: Mmmmm, some honor-filled roles. And how about serving up some service roles?

JON: Sue, I think we should just order a few of everything.

POPS: Now you're on a roll! Honey, get them at least one of everything!

MOM: You can stop by every day and pick up more. We never seem to run out.

SUE: We'll be back, that's for sure. And we'll tell our friends about you.

JON: By the way, I almost forgot why Mom and Dad sent us here—do you have any jelly rolls?

POPS: Jelly rolls? Hmmmm. Never thought of that!

MOM: No, we don't have any jelly rolls. Anyway, I can't imagine those catching on! I think we'll just stick with parental roles. They're the sensible food!

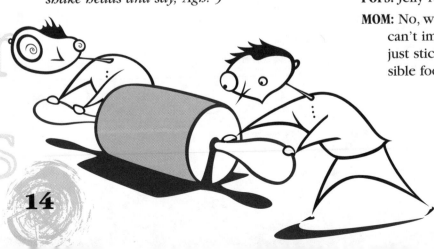

Bible Study

In contrast to the worldly authority of the Roman Empire, Jesus teaches His disciples about authority. He shares this teaching just before facing death on the cross for the sins of the world. Read Matthew 20:17–28.

1. According to verses 17–19, how did Jesus show that He was a servant?

2. What did the mom in this story think Jesus' kingdom was?

3. Is there anything wrong with her wanting the best for her sons? Explain.

4. In what way are your father and mother wanting the best for you by having you in confirmation study?

5. Can you give an example of someone you know who by serving in a special way demonstrates the love of God and helps motivate others to follow Him?

6. Can anyone keep God's Law completely? Why or why not?

7. What does the servant-leadership of Jesus mean for you personally? See 20:28.

Family in Faith Journal

Recall an injury or illness and the care your parent gave you during the healing process. Your parent or mentor should record this memory in your Family in Faith Journal.

Fun for Review

Characters: Teacher, Manny, Peggy, Lyn, Willie, Anita, Rick

Setting: Classroom

TEACHER: We're going to work on our assignment as a group. I want you to make a poster with an acrostic.

MANNY: I like doing acrostic puzzles.

PEGGY: Do you mean crossword puzzles?

LYN: An acrostic is when you put a word down the side of the page and each letter stands for something that has to do with that word.

TEACHER: That's right, Lyn.

WILLIE: What is the word we are going to use?

TEACHER: I want you to consider how we are to respect authorities God has placed over us—especially in our church and also in the government.

ANITA: Sometimes it's hard to respect people in government.

RICK: Sometimes it's hard to respect anyone! But I like it when people respect me.

TEACHER: The acrostic word is going to be "R-E-S-P-E-C-T." How and what do we respect in our church and government leaders?

MANNY: Let's start with the letter "R."

LYN: I know— "Rules." God gave the government to rule over us. And the government gives us lots of rules.

PEGGY: And there are rules in church too.

WILLIE: Yeah, like not falling asleep during the sermon. Pastor caught me last week!

ANITA: We need to respect the rules of the government …

RICK: Unless they go against God's rules.

MANNY: Okay, we have "R." What about "E"?

WILLIE: I know! "E" could stand for "Emportant." Church and government are emportant.

PEGGY: I hate to spoil your enthusiasm, but the word "Important" is spelled with an "I," not an "E"!

LYN: How about the word "Encourage"? We respect those in authority by encouraging. They really do have tough jobs.

WILLIE: And we all like to be encouraged in what we are doing.

ANITA: I think for "S" we could use the word "Servant," since pastors and other church workers are servants and people working in government are public servants.

RICK: And I'm ready for "P." Actually, there are three words— "Parents, Pastors, and Politicians." All are people God has placed in authority over us.

ANITA: I like that. Good job!

PEGGY: "E" can stand for "Education." We should respect the education of our leaders, and we should educate ourselves about their work and ministry so we can appreciate them more.

WILLIE: "C" could stand for "Calling." That is spelled with a "C" and not a "K," right?

MANNY: You're learning, Willie, my man!

LYN: They have a calling to serve God and us and we have a calling to respect their work.

WILLIE: This isn't a very fun one, but it can be used when talking about government— "T" could stand for "Taxes."

PEGGY: The Bible does talk about paying our taxes to the authorities.

ANITA: Maybe we could also use the word "Together." God wants us to work together with all whom He has placed in authority over us.

MANNY: That's it. We're finished! That was easy!

WILLIE: Easy? I don't know about you, but I thought that was a very **taxing** assignment!

Fifth Commandment 5

Table Talk

According to the catechism's explanation of the Fifth Commandment, how did the decisions of this family contradict God's Word?

How do Nicholas's actions show a clear understanding of the Fifth Commandment?

How does the true story of St. Nicholas contrast with modern tales of Santa Claus?

Bible Study

The road from Jerusalem to Jericho curves through rocky terrain where robbers can easily hide. Read Luke 10:25–37.

1. According to Old Testament law, priests and Levites were considered "unclean" for several days if they touched a dead man. They could not do their religious work. Would that have made it right for the men to pass by? Explain.

2. Sometimes robbers pretended to be beaten up. When a person stopped to help, the robber would leap up and rob them. Would that have been a good reason to pass by the man in the parable?

3. Considering that the Jews and Samaritans hated each other, what unusual twist does Jesus put into His parable? See Luke 10:33–35.

4. According to Jesus, who is our neighbor and what would God have us do for him? See Luke 10:36–37.

5. Name someone in your school who needs help. Who needs a special friend? Who needs some special words of encouragement?

6. How do abortion, euthanasia, and suicide violate the Fifth Commandment?

7. Motivated by God's love for those in need, what specifically might I do for someone this week? (Mentors should help to come up with several suggestions.)

8. We cannot keep God's Law perfectly. But who has kept the Law perfectly for us and our salvation?

9. How is Jesus similar to the Good Samaritan?

Family in Faith Journal

Recall an injury or illness and the care your parent gave you during the healing process. Your parent or mentor should record this memory in the Family in Faith Journal.

Fun for Review

Prop: Newspaper

Characters: Evil Angel, Good Angel, Man, 2 or 3 Thieves, Priest, Levite, Good Samaritan

Setting: The two ANGELS stand next to each other. The MAN is walking on a road, reading a newspaper.

EVIL ANGEL: *(Sneering)* Okay, this is going to be good! Watch what happens.

GOOD ANGEL: *(Wincing and shuddering)* You really shouldn't … I mean, you're really sick!

MAN: *(Mumbling to himself)* Hmmm, it says here, "Watch out for thieves on Jericho Way." Whew! At least I'm not on … wait a minute … yikes!

THIEVES rob him, then exit.

GOOD ANGEL: Wait! I see someone coming in the distance. The way he's dressed … it must be … wait a minute … it is! It's a priest. This man of God will surely help this poor fellow.

The PRIEST quickly passes by.

EVIL ANGEL: There goes your chance, choirboy. And to think only moments ago he was leading people in worship! That's my kind of priest!

GOOD ANGEL: Here comes a blessing! If the priest wouldn't help him, maybe this Levite will. He surely knows God's will. He surely knows to love thy neighbor.

The LEVITE passes by.

EVIL ANGEL: He surely knows how to keep walkin', baby! Yeah, baby! Keep walkin'! *(Laughing)*

GOOD SAMARITAN enters.

GOOD ANGEL: Hmmm. A Samaritan, huh? Samaritans and Jews usually hate each other. I wonder … I just wonder …

EVIL ANGEL: *(Listening to GOOD ANGEL)* You wonder what? You wonder if you're going to lose your job? *(Evil laugh)*

GOOD ANGEL: No. No, I don't. I wonder if the Lord … yep. I wouldn't put it past Him. This is the way He works sometimes, you know.

GOOD SAMARITAN sees the MAN and goes over to help him.

GOOD ANGEL: Thank You, Lord, for saving him. *(Turning to EVIL ANGEL)* And YOU! You little pointy-tail, pitch-fork, devil wannabe! You didn't think it was possible, did you? *(Mocking)* Noooo. Certainly not this Samaritan! Noooo. I guess you forgot about God's words, "Hear, O Israel, the Lord our God, the Lord is one. Love the Lord your God with all your heart and with all your soul and with all your mind and with all your strength." AND, "Love your neighbor as yourself. There is no commandment greater than these."

EVIL ANGEL: I'm mellllllllltiiiiiiing!

GOOD ANGEL: Now get outta here!

EVIL ANGEL: *(Looking into the distance)* Hey! Looks like they're going into an inn. Like he's gonna have enough to pay for all the help that guy needs.

GOOD ANGEL: I put a Visa card in his pocket.

EVIL ANGEL: A what?

GOOD ANGEL: Just give it up, would ya?!

Bible Study

King David rules Israel. Instead of leading his men, David stays at the palace and falls into temptation. Read 2 Samuel 11:1-15, 26-27.

1. What sexual sin did David commit?

2. In what way is this story like a snowball rolling down a large hill of fresh, sticky snow? Read James 1:15. How was David's sin much like the description given by James?

3. Can you describe a time when some small, sinful desire took over your life and became bigger and bigger with time?

4. How might the Sixth Commandment apply to homosexuality and pornography?

5. List everything you learned in this lesson about God's gift of sexuality. Circle the one fact you did not know before you came to class. Underline the one thing on the list you think you might someday have the most difficulty obeying. Explain why.

6. Read David's confession of his sin with Bathsheba as recorded in Psalm 51:10–12. Where do we also find forgiveness for the sexual sins we commit?

7. Does having God's forgiveness mean that the consequences of our sin immediately go away? Read 2 Samuel 12:13–14.

8. No matter how hard we try, we fail to keep our hearts and thoughts pure from lust. Who alone can keep this commandment purely and take away our sin?

Family in Faith Journal

Your parent or mentor should describe how they first met their spouse and fell in love. What place does God's love have in that relationship? Summarize the story in the Family in Faith Journal.

Fun for Review

Characters: Big Brother, Little Brother, Bird, Bee

Setting: Family Room

BIG BROTHER: *(Motioning to chair)* Little brother, have a seat. It's time we had a little talk.

LITTLE BROTHER: *(Sitting down)* Oh, no. I don't like the sound of this.

BIG BROTHER: *(Pacing back and forth)* Well, it's time we had this talk.

LITTLE BROTHER: You said that already, big brother.

BIG BROTHER: I did? Oh, yeah. I'm just a little nervous. Well. The talk. Ummm. Little brother …

LITTLE BROTHER: Yes?

BIG BROTHER: I want to talk to you about the, ummm …

LITTLE BROTHER: Yes?

BIG BROTHER: Well, you're getting older now, and you need to know about the birds and the bees.

LITTLE BROTHER: *(Softly mumbling)* Oh, I should have known—the sex talk.

BIG BROTHER: What's that, little brother?

LITTLE BROTHER: Umm, I said I should have taken Rex for a walk.

BIG BROTHER: I just took him out. Besides, I want to have this talk about the birds and the bees.

LITTLE BROTHER: Okay, okay … the birds and the bees.

BIG BROTHER: It goes like this … *(BIG BROTHER paces and pretends to be talking to LITTLE BROTHER as the BIRD and BEE do their part.)*

BIRD: *(Flies into room)* Tweet. Tweet. Tweet.

BEE: *(Flies into room)* Buzzz. Buzzzz. Buzzzz.

BIRD: Cheep. Cheep.

BEE: Hmmmmmm. Hmmmmmm.

BIRD: Cheep. Cheep. Tweet. Tweet.

BEE: Buzzzz. Buzzz. Buzzz. Sting!

BIG BROTHER: And that's what I wanted to tell you.

LITTLE BROTHER: *(Sarcastic)* That's, well, what should I say? That's very helpful, big brother.

BIG BROTHER: I'm glad, little brother.

LITTLE BROTHER: I was being sarcastic. That didn't help me at all.

BIG BROTHER: Oh?

LITTLE BROTHER: Mom and Dad already talked with me about sex. You don't have to disguise the subject by using birds and bees. I know that it's a wonderful gift from God. It's an emotional and physical gift to be shared joyfully only within marriage. Within relationships, a man and a woman need to respect each other and keep Christ their focus as they grow together in His love.

BIG BROTHER: What?! They told you already?

LITTLE BROTHER: I also learned about sex in confirmation, in a short story told by a German shepherd.

BIG BROTHER: A German shepherd? And you thought the birds and bees were out of line?

LITTLE BROTHER: Here's what the German shepherd says: "We should fear and love God so that we lead a sexually pure and decent life in what we say and do, and husband and wife love and honor each other."

BIG BROTHER: Wait a minute. That's what Martin Luther wrote about the Sixth Commandment.

LITTLE BROTHER: Right! Luther was a German shepherd—a German pastor. "Pastor" means shepherd.

BIG BROTHER: And the "German shepherd" told us what the Bible says about sex and relationships. I still like the birds and the bees.

BIRD: *(Flies into room)* Tweet. Tweet. Tweet.

BEE: *(Flies into room)* Buzzz. Buzzzz. Buzzzz.

BIRD: Cheep. Cheep.

BEE: Hmmmmmm. Hmmmmmm.

Table of Duties, Home and Work

Bible Study

Ruth and Naomi's husbands have died. They are poor and face severe hardship, even starvation. Read Ruth 2:2–23; 4:9–10.

1. What did Boaz quickly recognize in Ruth? See 2:11–12.

2. Contrast Ruth's care for her mother-in-law with what happens in today's society with many destitute people. What programs are in place to help them? What about in your church?

3. Why is Ruth 1:16–17 such a great summary of the whole story of the Book of Ruth?

4. Who in your family or other relationships is loyal to you like Ruth was to her mother-in-law? How have you been blessed through their loyalty and love for you?

5. What do husband and wife promise to do in their marriage vows? What does this teach about divorce?

6. Sin tears at every family. Who alone can rescue your family from division?

7. Since God is our heavenly Father, what does that mean for our families?

Family in Faith Journal

Studies tell us that many people do not have a purpose in life. They don't know why they're here on earth. They don't know if life has any meaning. With your parent or mentor, write out your purpose and reason for living as a child of God in Christ.

Fun for Review

Characters: Cissy (4 years old), Bobby (3 years old)

Setting: Anywhere

(The sketch will be enhanced if characters talk and act like little children.)

CISSY: Bobby, what are you going to be when you grow up?

BOBBY: I'm not gonna grow up. I'm always gonna be three.

CISSY: You have to grow up.

BOBBY: Do not!

CISSY: Do too! *If* you grow up, what do you want to be?

BOBBY: I'm gonna drive the big truck that picks up our garbage.

CISSY: That's a stinky job.

BOBBY: You're stinky!

CISSY: Am not!

BOBBY: Are too! There's nothing wrong with drivin' the big truck. I bet when you grow up, you'll be happy to see me take away your trash. Otherwise your whole yard and house will be stinky. Without me, you'll be a stinky family with stinky garbage.

CISSY: Will not!

BOBBY: Will too! Stinky! Stinky! Stinky!

CISSY: Okay, I guess that's a 'portant job. I don't want to stink up my house with trash.

BOBBY: What kind of job are you going to have?

CISSY: I'm going to be a mommy.

BOBBY: A mommy? That's not a real job.

CISSY: Is too! My mom works hard. She takes care of me. She loves me and my daddy. Mommy work isn't easy. My mom cooks, drives me places, plays games with me, and even cleans the bathroom.

BOBBY: She likes doing that?

CISSY: She likes being a mommy, and that's what I want to be. Just like my mommy or … maybe a ballerina.

BOBBY: Are you going to get married to a boy?

CISSY: Sounds yucky, but I guess I will have to. I'm not going to like being around boys until I'm like, really old. You know … 30 or 40.

BOBBY: Boys aren't yucky. Girls are.

CISSY: Are not!

BOBBY: Are too!

(Pause.)

BOBBY: I think I'm going to pick up some trash around the house. That will be good practice for when I clean with the big truck someday.

CISSY: And I think I'll practice being a mommy.

BOBBY: Okay.

CISSY: Hey, why do we have to be anything at all? Do I have to work?

BOBBY: Sure! Everyone has to work, 'cause God made it that way. 'Member what He said to Adam and Eve? They had to take care of the garden.

CISSY: I 'member … and they had to get married and have babies too.

BOBBY: That's *really* yucky!

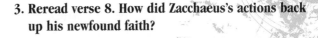

Table Talk

How do shoplifters affect your life?

If a friend asked you to help him/her shoplift, what might you say?

Is it okay to steal if you really need something? Explain.

How does stealing show a lack of fear and trust for God?

Bible Study

As a tax collector, Zacchaeus demands more taxes from the people in his region so that he can make himself rich. Jesus visits Zacchaeus's community and preaches about God's kingdom. Read Luke 19:1–10.

1. How did Zacchaeus's actions break the Seventh Commandment?

2. If Zacchaeus used the money he collected for a worthy cause, would that make everything okay? Explain.

3. Reread verse 8. How did Zacchaeus's actions back up his newfound faith?

4. Share a time with one another when you felt repentant for something you had done and tried to make up for the wrongdoing in a way similar to Zacchaeus.

5. Though some were angry with Jesus for going to Zacchaeus's house, what did Jesus teach them about His mission?

6. Why are you personally glad Jesus came to seek and to save sinners?

Family in Faith Journal

List things you share at home. Make a second list of things you don't share and discuss with your parent or mentor why you don't. Talk about how Jesus would have us use our possessions. Record these thoughts in the Family in Faith Journal.

Fun for Review

Characters: 3 Complainers, Zacchaeus, Jesus

Setting: ZACCHAEUS walks by on his way to his tax booth. He takes a seat and begins counting coins. COMPLAINERS stand nearby.

COMPLAINER 1: (*Sarcastically*) Well, there goes his "excellency," Zacchaeus the Zucchini.

COMPLAINER 2: How much do you owe him this time?

COMPLAINER 1: About 50 denarii! That's not nearly as much as it used to be, but it's still too much.

COMPLAINER 3: Whatever happened to old Zucchini, anyway? Why the sudden change in tax policy? Is he trying to trick us somehow?

COMPLAINER 1: Didn't you hear? He's got religion. Remember when Jesus passed through town, preaching about the kingdom of God? He stayed at Zucchini's house. He's been acting suspiciously ever since.

COMPLAINER 2: Yeah. He gave back some of my tax money. And he gave four times as much to Widow Sarah. Ever since he met Jesus, he's been smiling and friendly. He's gone through a big change.

COMPLAINER 1: But he's still a "wee little man" in my eyes! People don't change like that. Zucchini's up to something. He'll squash every tax dollar out of us that he can.

ALL COMPLAINERS: (*Turn toward ZACCHAEUS and shake fists.*) Squasher! (*Exit singing "Zucchini was a wee little man."*)

ZACCHAEUS: (*Looking sad*) When I charged too much for taxes, they didn't trust me. Now that I've repaid people, they're still suspicious. Why do I even bother?

JESUS: (*Enters behind ZACCHAEUS*) You bother because your stealing bothered Me.

ZACCHAEUS: (*Surprised*) Jesus?

JESUS: And your stealing didn't just bother Me. It bothered others as well. Think about Widow Sarah. Because of high taxes, she had nothing to feed her children.

ZACCHAEUS: Yeah, I remember, nothing but squash!

JESUS: And your other neighbors, aren't they better off now?

ZACCHAEUS: (*Growing cheerful*) Yes, now they have extra money to improve and protect their possessions and income. Everyone's better off. (*Growing sad*) Everyone but me.

JESUS: God's commandments aren't just about you, Zach. They're about everyone. Before we met, you only thought of yourself and your possessions. Now that you fear and love God, you care about your neighbors as well. Not everyone understands yet. But give them some time to see the difference God can make.

ALL COMPLAINERS: (*Enter singing*) Zucchini was a wee little man and a wee little man was he!

COMPLAINER 1: (*Interrupting*) Hey! Isn't that Jesus talking with Zucchini again?

COMPLAINER 3: I wonder what they're up to. Probably some new tax scheme. I hear that Jesus wants to start a kingdom of His own. He probably needs the money.

ALL COMPLAINERS: (*Turn toward ZACCHAEUS and JESUS, shaking fists.*) Squashers! (*Exit.*)

JESUS: Well, Zach, since I came to seek and to save the lost, it looks like I have some more work to do. (*Calling after COMPLAINERS*) Wait up! Let Me tell you about a kingdom without taxes.

Eighth Commandment

Table Talk

How did Nick Nickolson's dishonesty affect the lives of other people?

Do you think people will trust Nick Nicholson again? Why?

Is it possible to tell lies and never get caught?

Bible Study

Just before His arrest, Jesus stays at the home of Simon, a Pharisee. Mary enters the room unexpectedly and anoints Him. Read Mark 14:3–11.

1. Why did Jesus welcome Mary's action? See 14:7–9.

2. How do the thoughts of some of the people go against the Eighth Commandment?

3. Share with one another insulting words that have been spoken to you that have stayed with you over the years (e.g., shrimp, fatso, homo). How did these words make you feel? What kind of words have you spoken to others in the last week that you wish you could take back?

4. What words might cheer up someone who is having a bad day?

5. Give an example of how you might defend someone's reputation this week. How might you speak up for someone this week?

6. Reread verse 8. In what way did Jesus' life, death, burial, and resurrection rescue us from those words we've spoken that have been unkind and have hurt other people?

7. As a sinner, how does the way Jesus spoke to Mary encourage you?

Family in Faith Journal

Your parent or mentor will come up with five specific compliments for you. Record these compliments in the Family in Faith Journal.

Fun for Review

Characters: Editor, Reporter 1, Reporter 2, Reporter 3

Setting: Staff meeting of The National Informant

EDITOR: So, staff, what story ideas do we have for the special school issue of *The National Informant*?

REPORTER 1: I spent the week at the junior high school on the west side of town.

EDITOR: What do you have?

REPORTER 1: I heard some girls talking about another chick in their class who they say stole some earrings. It sounds like she's a straight "A" student and they want her to get in trouble. She's smart but ugly. The way they talked, no one liked her.

EDITOR: Did you talk to anyone else, or are you just taking their word for it?

REPORTER 1: I don't know anything for sure, but who cares?

REPORTER 2: Well, I spent time at a different junior high school. I heard some students at a lunch table laughing about a teacher they can't stand. I think they said something about him going to a shrink three times a week. He's probably psycho!

EDITOR: Are you sure they said "shrink"? Maybe he's a skater and goes to the "rink" three times a week. You know you don't hear very well.

REPORTER 2: Shrink … rink. Who cares?

EDITOR: Okay, what else do we have?

REPORTER 3: I spent the last couple of days at this Christian school. Talk about bizarre stories.

EDITOR: Tell us!

REPORTER 3: The teachers were telling the kids about some baby born of a virgin! Great headline material, huh? But that's not all. I guess the parents are really poor and don't have insurance, so they keep the baby in a barn. Get this—the baby sleeps in a feeding trough for the animals!

REPORTER 2: Good scoop, Scooter!

EDITOR: I'm not so sure about this. What else did you hear?

REPORTER 3: It seems this baby grows up. People make fun of Him, make up lies about Him, betray and slander Him, and try to hurt His reputation. But it doesn't end there—they kill Him. And while He's dying, He forgives the people who kill Him!

EDITOR: This is too bizarre!

REPORTER 3: The way I overheard it, this guy dies out of love for others, hoping that as He loved them, they will love one another. So that instead of lying and ruining people's reputations, they will explain everything in the kindest way and not slander and …

EDITOR: Okay, we've heard enough of that garbage. I know we've done some wild stories, but this is too wild.

REPORTER 2: Like that one where the alien with only a head gives birth to a laptop computer.

REPORTER 1: Hey, that was one of my best stories!

EDITOR: Let's go with the story about the girl who stole the earrings for the cover story. But you don't have any reliable sources?

REPORTER 1: Since when did we care about reliable sources? When did we begin caring about hurting someone's feelings or reputation?

EDITOR: Good point. Let's go with it. And then let's follow up with the story about the teacher. Add some stuff that makes them both look really bad, okay?

REPORTERS 1 and 2: You can count on us, boss. You can count on us.

Ninth and Tenth Commandments

Table Talk

How were the desires of Boniface and the Frisian tribesmen different?

How did the thoughts of Boniface and the tribesmen change their actions?

If you scheme to get what belongs to someone else but never carry out your plan, have you broken the Ninth or Tenth Commandments? Explain.

Bible Study

Ahab is king of Samaria and Naboth is one of his subjects. Read 1 Kings 21.

1. Was it wrong for Ahab to want to buy Naboth's vineyard? When did Ahab begin to sin?

2. In what way does verse 5 reflect how some people act when they don't get what they want?

3. Can you name a time when you sulked over something you didn't get?

4. What happened when you sulked? Did you get what you wanted?

5. Define in your own words the meaning of "coveting." Give some personal examples of when you've coveted.

6. Reread 21:28–29. Why might God bring punishment for Ahab's sin on the next generation?

7. Read or recall the opening words of Psalm 23. Where can you find true contentment?

8. How might knowing Christ grant you contentment?

Family in Faith Journal

Record a time when you really wanted something and didn't get it (e.g., a Christmas present). How might you see things differently now in light of the commandments and the life of Jesus? Ask your parent or mentor to record the experience in the Family in Faith Journal.

Fun for Review

Props: Pirate's patches for Ahab and Jezebel, paper and pen/pencil

Characters: Narrator, Naboth, Ahab, Jezebel, Elders, Nobles

Setting: NABOTH is looking over his vineyard with admiration.

NARRATOR: This is the story about a king who didn't get what he wanted … and he pitched a royal fit! *(Turning dramatically)* Now, behold Naboth admiring his vineyards!

NABOTH: Wow, these vines are awesome! And look at how healthy these grapes are! I have a wonderful vineyard. Thank You, Lord.

NARRATOR: Here comes the king.

AHAB: *(AHAB approaches NABOTH with royal pride. Speaking with a royal tone)* Behold the presence of your king, Mr. Naboth. *(NABOTH goes to his knees in reverence. AHAB holds down his hand to have NABOTH kiss his ring. NABOTH thinks AHAB is offering a hand to help him up. He takes it and rises to his feet.)*

NABOTH: Thanks, your highness. *(AHAB looks disgusted and wipes off his hand.)*

AHAB: *(Still with disgust)* Don't mention it. *(Changing tone back to royal status; clears throat)* Say, my good fellow. You have a rather awesome vineyard. I should be happy to own such a piece of land. I shall pay you hand-somely for it—whatever it takes. Just give me your "yes," Naboth.

NABOTH: No, your highness.

AHAB: No, Naboth. *Yes!*

NABOTH: Yes, your highness, but *no!*

AHAB: You mean *yes.*

NABOTH: No, I mean "no." Sorry, your highness.

NARRATOR: King Ahab leaves Naboth and returns to his palace home, where his wife Jezebel is waiting.

(ELDERS and NOBLES are at the front and bow as AHAB passes into his home. AHAB acknowledges them properly, but as soon as he gets home he pitches a fit.)

JEZEBEL: Oh, hi, honey-pots! How'd it go?

AHAB: *(Stomping up and down like a spoiled child)* Oooohhh, drat! Double-drat! Mashed potatoes! *(Starting to cry)* I WANT NABOTH'S VINEYARD! I WANT IT! I WANT IT! I WANT IT!

JEZEBEL: It's okay, my little pookie-poo, kingie-wingie. If you want his vineyard, you'll get his vineyard! Now go wash up; it's almost time for dinner.

(Like a little child sulking, AHAB leaves the room.)

NARRATOR: And so the spoiled boy who would be king—I mean spoiled King Ahab—went to wash up for dinner. Meanwhile, his lovely wife—albeit a conniving wife—the first lady, Jezebel, comes up with a great, yet wicked idea.

JEZEBEL: *(Taking up paper and pen/pencil)* I have a great, yet wicked idea!

NARRATOR: She writes a letter, puts the king's official seal of approval on it, and gives it to the elders and nobles—to give to the elders and nobles in Naboth's land.

28

Close of the Commandments **11**

Table Talk

Do good intentions always bring good results? Explain your answer.

Do doctors and nurses want to hurt or heal their patients?

How does God's Law work like medicine?

How does the Gospel work like medicine?

Bible Study

In a previous lesson we read about David's sin with Bathsheba. Today's Bible story describes how the prophet Nathan confronts David with his sin. Read 2 Samuel 12:1-20.

1. What made Nathan's job difficult?

2. If you were Nathan and you had a friend who had sinned, what kind of illustration might you use to help him see his sin? Use the same format Nathan used (verses 1–4), only update it by changing the characters.

3. Name a time when you felt like David feels in verses 7–10. Did you feel frightened? ashamed? guilty?

4. Identify where the Law is forcefully proclaimed in the story.

5. Identify how Nathan proclaims the Gospel of God's forgiveness.

6. How do David's actions show that he truly feared, loved, and trusted in God?

7. Read together Colossians 1:13–14 in celebration of the forgiveness that is yours through Jesus Christ. What part of this passage do you find most striking?

Family in Faith Journal

When parents show us our mistakes, they act like God applying His Law. When parents forgive us, they act like God applying the Gospel. Recall a time when your parents forgave you. Record the event in the Family in Faith Journal.

Fun for Review

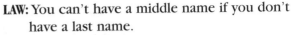

Props: 3 chairs

Characters: Matchmaker, a male and a female to play Law and Gospel

Setting: TV studio

MATCHMAKER: Hi, everyone! Welcome to the show everyone is talking about—"Matches Made in Heaven." I'm the Matchmaker, and tonight we have a true match made in heaven. First, let's give a big welcome to … Law!

(Everyone claps.)

LAW: *(Enters; sits to the right of MATCHMAKER)* Thank you. It's good to be here.

MATCHMAKER: We're excited to introduce you to what should be a match made in heaven. Before we meet your match, tell us, where are you from?

LAW: I grew up on Mount Sinai. It's definitely God's country. But I was first revealed in a garden.

MATCHMAKER: I understand that now you are a world traveler?

LAW: That's correct.

MATCHMAKER: Well, you have that in common with your match made in heaven, whom we want to bring out now. Come on out, Gospel! Let's show Gospel some love by putting our hands together.

(All clap. GOSPEL enters. MATCHMAKER and LAW stand. GOSPEL sits on the other side of MATCHMAKER.)

GOSPEL: You are so gracious. Thank you.

MATCHMAKER: I understand *you* are the gracious one.

GOSPEL: Well, grace is my middle name.

LAW: You can't have a middle name if you don't have a last name.

MATCHMAKER: Good point, Law. Anyway, where are you from?

GOSPEL: I'm much older than I look. I'm eternal. I was first announced as a promise to a couple named Adam and Eve.

MATCHMAKER: And since then you've been carried into the world, correct?

GOSPEL: That's right. I use my gifts wherever I'm proclaimed. It keeps me busy, but I love what I do.

MATCHMAKER: Let's learn a little about what each of you do for a living. Law, let's start with you.

LAW: I show people their sins. I set down rules and guidelines. I look them in the eyes and show them where they have failed. Part of my time is also spent acting as a kind of curb so people aren't doing whatever they want to do. In addition, I guide believers in the way they are to live as God's forgiven people in Christ.

MATCHMAKER: That job must keep you busy! *(LAW nods.)* So, Gospel, tell us what you do.

GOSPEL: My name means "Good News," and that tells my work. I love bringing the Good News to people who have met up with Law. You see, Law, you may not have realized it, but I've been following you around for a long time.

LAW: What? Really?

GOSPEL: You show people their sins, and I show them their Savior. I get to tell them that there is hope through the forgiveness of their sins. Jesus came to die for them and to save them from their sins. I share Jesus' love, His promises, and all of His Good News.

LAW: I thought that since we were total opposites, we'd never be a match, but it's just the opposite.

MATCHMAKER: You need each other. Without Law there would be no need for Gospel. And who would need to hear the Gospel's message if they didn't know Law? This truly is a match made in heaven! Well, that's our show for tonight!

Table of Duties, Calling throughout Life

Table Talk

As Romans 13:9 shows, love for our neighbor is always based on God's love for our neighbors. According to 2 Peter 3:9, what does God desire for your neighbors?

Bible Study

Everywhere Jesus looked, He saw men and women who were "like sheep without a shepherd" (Matthew 9:36). Determined to multiply His ministry, He sent His disciples out to help with the work. He warned that the work of discipleship would often meet with resistance, even from within one's own family. Read Matthew 9:35–38 and 10:37–42.

1. If Jesus asked you to help Him care for other people, how might you respond?

2. How might your response change in view of Matthew 10:37–39?

3. What does "taking up the cross" (Matthew 10:38) indicate might happen as we carry out our God-given purpose in life?

4. If a leader at your church encouraged you to become a pastor, deaconess, director of Christian education, teacher, or missionary, what might you say?

5. In what way is Matthew 9:37–38 as true today as it was when Jesus spoke the words?

6. Do you have to be a trained church worker to share God's Word with others?

7. Discuss with your parent/mentor his or her job. How does this job show love and care for other people?

8. Point out where the story proclaims the Law and the Gospel.

9. What was Jesus' calling and what does it mean for your life?

Family in Faith Journal

Though Christians have individual callings as parents or children, we all have a common calling according to Romans 13:9 and 1 Timothy 2:1. From these two verses, write God's common calling for your life in your Family in Faith Journal.

Fun for Review

Prop: Phone (if not available, pantomime)

Characters: Sarah, Voice of Jesus (over the phone)

Setting: Sarah's home

(Sound of phone ringing)

SARAH: *(Answering phone)* Hello?

JESUS: Sarah, how are you?

SARAH: Jesus—it's You!

JESUS: You know My voice. I wrote in My book that My sheep—My children—know My voice.

SARAH: And You called me by name.

JESUS: You are mine, Sarah. You are My child, whom I love.

SARAH: I love You too, Jesus.

JESUS: Did you enjoy the day I shared with you today?

SARAH: It was great, thanks. Great job on the sunset! And thanks for Your help on the history test.

JESUS: I'm pretty good with history, aren't I?

SARAH: By the way, is this a long distance call?

JESUS: It is long distance; well, actually, it's about a long distance call.

SARAH: I haven't made any long distance calls lately.

JESUS: I'm not talking about a phone call.

SARAH: You're confusing me, Jesus.

JESUS: I wanted to remind you about the long distance call you have, Sarah.

SARAH: This one?

JESUS: Remember, it's not a phone call … it's about My calling you to stick with Me for the long haul. I'm sticking with you, Sarah. I will always be there for you and I have great plans for you.

SARAH: So You're talking about the idea of You calling me to be Your child for a long distance—through this earthly life and into heaven one day.

JESUS: You've got the idea!

SARAH: Sometimes I think I'm not all that important, Jesus. I'm sorry for that.

JESUS: You're forgiven! You're special!

SARAH: And You want to use me somehow?

JESUS: There are lots of people that will be coming in and out of your life that don't know about Me. I want you to tell them about Me.

SARAH: But I'm always afraid I'll say the wrong thing.

JESUS: I'm going to give you the words to say. Remember that little girl you helped on the playground last week? You were great with her.

SARAH: I never imagined that You were behind that. I *did* know what to say and do. You're awesome!

JESUS: So are you!

SARAH: Thanks for calling me today and thanks for calling me through Baptism. You have given me a real long distance call. With Your help, I'll make it to the end!

JESUS: Sounds like a great plan. You can count on Me. Don't be afraid to tell others about Me. Use the phone if you want. You're very comfortable talking on the phone.

SARAH: That's what all my friends say! Thanks! You're a great problem solver in more ways than one! Should I say good-bye or Amen?

JESUS: Let's just keep talking … phone or no phone. Remember, this is a long distance call without long distance charges!

Apostles' Creed, First Article A

Table Talk

Based on the story of Copernicus, can Christians be good scientists? Explain your answer.

Are scientists always right? Give examples.

Science is based on observing facts and reporting those facts. Who observed the origins of the universe?

The human brain has 30 billion nerve cells. In order for you to sit here today, billions of these cells must work with other cells with exact timing. Your brain sends out messages to over 200 muscles just for you to sit down. How could this happen by mere accident, or chance, as the evolutionists suggest?

Bible Study

After Jesus grows up, God calls John the Baptist to prepare the way for Jesus' ministry of salvation. Read Matthew 3.

1. If God created a perfect world, then why did people need John the Baptist's ministry of repentance?

2. Briefly describe John's preaching. What does it tell you about how the Creator feels about His creation?

3. What happened when Jesus was baptized?

4. What three divine persons were heard or seen at Jesus' Baptism?

5. The word "trinity" or "triune" means three (tri-) in one (-une). How does this story reveal God's threefold nature?

6. How does this story reveal the Creator's power over creation? His love for creation?

7. Contrast John's preaching with the heavenly Father's words in 3:17. How do these passages show the Law and Gospel character of God?

Family in Faith Journal

Take a tour of the sanctuary and identify as many symbols of the Trinity as you can find. Choose your favorite and sketch it in the Family in Faith Journal.

Fun for Review

Characters: Bobby, Billy, Amy, Suzy, various people to make background animal noises

Setting: Zoo

(Zoo noises are heard, but die off when dialogue begins.)

BOBBY: Look at these animals!

BILLY: *(Mockingly)* Ooooh! Animals. I'm so impressed!

AMY: Oh, Billy! Don't be such a cynic!

BOBBY: A what?

SUZY: She means someone who doesn't appreciate God's creation … or everything that He provides for us.

BOBBY: Look at all of the different kinds of animals! God is so amazing!

(An animal noise is made as each animal is named.)

AMY: Look, a Clydesdale horse!

SUZY: Sheep!

BOBBY: An elephant!

BILLY: Okay, I guess I like that rattlesnake over there.

AMY: Hey, a gazelle!

SUZY: Hmmm, I never knew a gazelle made a noise like that.

BILLY: And you guys think God made these animals? I think they're all products of an evolutionary process that probably started on the Galapagos Islands about a *billion* years ago.

AMY: Oh, Billy, Billy, Billy. You can't possibly tell me you believe that all of this is just some quirk of nature?

(A duck quacks.)

BILLY: She said, "QUIRK"! *(The duck quacks again.)*

SUZY: And where do you think *we* came from, Billy?

BILLY: See that ring-tailed monkey over there? *(A monkey sounds.)*

BOBBY: Oh, come on, strong-willed Bill. You've said it in church and probably never even thought about what you were saying.

BILLY: Said what?

BOBBY: What do you think it means when we confess, "I believe in God, the Father Almighty, *MAKER* of heaven and earth"?

BILLY: There you go bringing God into the picture again. Keep it for Sunday, boys and girls.

SUZY: How can you look at this world and not think of Almighty God? I see beautiful mountains or a magnificent sunset and I say, "Thank You, Lord."

AMY: I see these animals and think to myself, "Wow, Lord! You've made some amazing creatures."

(All animal sounds chime in.)

BOBBY: I look at us! Everything God has blessed us with: our clothes, food, and, dare I say, even our parents?

AMY: Everything we need to support this life comes from God.

BILLY: Oh yeah? Well, I see a broken world—and animals that bite …

(Something growls. They all simultaneously take one step backward.)

BILLY: What did this poor loser of a world do to deserve all of this?

BOBBY: Actually a lot.

AMY and SUZY: Sin!

BILLY: Then why would God still provide all of those so-called beautiful things? What'd we do to deserve *that*?

BOBBY: Not a thing, bub.

AMY: Nope. Nothin'.

SUZY: It's called love.

BOBBY: It's called grace.

AMY: Admit it, Billy-boy, you've got a lot to be thankful for.

BILLY: Yeah, yeah. I suppose.

BOBBY: Hey, guys! Let's go look at that gazelle again. I think he's finally cleared his throat.

Apostles' Creed, First Article B

Table Talk

How is the theory of evolution a dangerous teaching?

Do you have to believe in evolution to be a good scientist? Defend your answer.

How does your belief in God affect the way you see other people?

If God is almighty, why do you think some people have a hard time believing that He simply created everything out of nothing through His Word?

Bible Study

After creating the earth, God personally creates the first people. Read Genesis 2.

1. In your own words, describe the Garden of Eden before humankind sinned.

2. Why are you glad God did something about man's loneliness? See 2:18–23.

3. What do you think God meant when He said the woman would be a "helper"?

4. Explain why Adam and Eve didn't wear clothes and yet were not ashamed. Contrast that scene to what it says in Genesis 3:10. What happened that brought about shame?

5. After Adam and Eve listened to Satan and rebelled, how did God promise to save them? See 3:15.

6. Point out where the story proclaims the Law and the Gospel.

Family in Faith Journal

Your parent or mentor will describe the wonder of a child's birth. Record this in the Family in Faith Journal.

Fun for Review

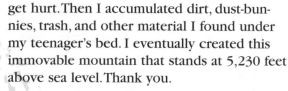

Prop: Sunglasses (if available)

Characters: Host, Heckler, Inventor 1 (male), Inventor 2 (female—wearing sunglasses), Inventor 3 (male), Judge

Setting: A convention center

HOST: Welcome to the impressively important inaugural International Invention Institution in Indianapolis, Indiana.

HECKLER: *(Offstage)* We can't hear you! And could you talk a little faster?

HOST: *(Faster and louder)* Welcome to the impressively important inaugural International Invention Institution in Indianapolis, Indiana.

HECKLER: Easy for you to say!

HOST: We have three finalists. Awards for these inventions will be based on creativity, usefulness, and lasting quality of workmanship.

HECKLER: Did anyone create a belly-button-lint remover?

HOST: No! Our first inventor made something that he couldn't actually bring in today. So if you'll take a look at the video screen, he'll tell you about his creation.

INVENTOR 1: Thank you. I made a mountain out of a molehill. As you can see on the screen, I began with a molehill approximately one foot high. I chased the mole out so he wouldn't get hurt. Then I accumulated dirt, dust-bunnies, trash, and other material I found under my teenager's bed. I eventually created this immovable mountain that stands at 5,230 feet above sea level. Thank you.

HOST: Let's give inventor number 1 a big hand. *(All clap.)*

HOST: Without further ado, let's bring up our second finalist.

INVENTOR 2: *(Pretending to roll a large, bright ball)* Hello! Sorry for the bright light. In fact, you may want to shade your eyes. I created a star. It started as a light bulb. I looked at the bulb and said, "Baby, you're going to be a star one day!"

HOST: Let's give a big hand for our second inventor while welcoming our last inventor.

(All clap.)

INVENTOR 3: I'm really embarrassed. I had a little problem coming to the convention hall today. I had created the perfect being. It had no fears and no shame, it never sinned, it always picked up its clothes, and it couldn't die. But I just found out that it could break. On the way here, it fell and broke. My original masterpiece isn't like it used to be. I couldn't even save it. Thanks for your time.

HOST: The judges are tallying their votes. *(Receives an envelope from JUDGE)* Ladies and gentlemen, I have the final vote. *(Opens envelope)* Oh, no! There's a problem. Our judges have disqualified all our contestants because their work isn't original. Here's a judge to explain.

JUDGE: It's obvious that each inventor stole his or her ideas from the greatest creator ever— God. God created the mountains, the stars, and the whole universe. And as for the perfect human being … hello? Has anyone read Genesis? Perfect humans, the fall, things aren't the same? The only thing different is that God *was* able to save His fallen creation through His Son, Jesus. This competition is a farce! Let's give God a hand for His creative work all around us!

(All clap.)

Apostles' Creed, Second Article A

Table Talk

Consider for a moment how God created the world, raised the dead, and was born of a virgin. How is it possible for Him to be both God and man?

How is the Bible's teaching that Jesus is true man a comfort to you?

Cults like the Mormons and the Jehovah's Witnesses don't believe that Jesus is truly God. Why is that important?

Bible Study

After hours of teaching and ministering to crowds of people, Jesus and His disciples sail across the Sea of Galilee. Read Mark 4:35–41.

1. Which part of the story shows that Jesus was human? Which part shows He was divine?

2. How do you think the disciples felt before and after the storm?

3. Name a time when you felt as the disciples must have felt before Jesus awoke.

4. Name a time when you felt like the disciples must have felt after Jesus stilled the storm.

5. What does Jesus' name literally mean? In your own words, tell another person how Jesus saved you.

6. In your own words, tell one another what it means to say, "I believe in Jesus Christ."

7. What do you confess about Jesus' conception and birth according to the Apostles' Creed?

Family in Faith Journal

Your parent or mentor will describe how they first learned about Jesus and how their understanding has changed over time. Record these memories in the Family in Faith Journal.

Fun for Review

Props: Chairs—to be arranged as seating in a boat with three chairs set up for Jesus to sleep on and a chair for Disciple 1 in front of everyone else's, like a captain's chair on a bridge; cushion or pillow

Characters: 6 Disciples, Jesus Christ

Setting: JESUS and the DISCIPLES are walking to the boat. JESUS is just finishing up explaining a parable.

DISCIPLES 3–6: TO THE OTHER SIDE!

DISCIPLE 1: *(Pointing ahead)* Engage!

DISCIPLE 2: Aye, aye, captain!

DISCIPLE 6: Do y'all see what I see?

DISCIPLES: *(With combined panic)* Yeah, we do.

DISCIPLE 1: Great! This is just great! Someone wake the Master.

DISCIPLE 2: Aye, captain, but He did say He needed some rest.

(DISCIPLES mimic a fierce storm [i.e., swaying back and forth].)

DISCIPLE 3: Oh, the wind!

DISCIPLE 4: Oh, the rain!

DISCIPLE 5: Oh, the waves!

DISCIPLE 6: Oh, I think I'm gonna be sick!

(With even greater panic)

DISCIPLE 2: Captain! She's breaking up! She's breaking up!

DISCIPLE 1: More power! We need more power!

DISCIPLE 3–6: WE-ARE-GOING-TO-DIE!

(Continue to make commotion and fierce storm sounds or whatever.)

DISCIPLE 1: Somebody! Somebody get to Jesus! Wake Him! Do it now!

DISCIPLE 2: Aye, captain! I think I can make it to the stern!

DISCIPLE 1: And quit saying, "Aye, captain"!

DISCIPLE 2: Aye, captain! I … I mean, sure! You got it, baby!

(DISCIPLE 2 makes his way to JESUS and shakes Him awake.)

DISCIPLE 2: Wake up! PLEASE wake up! Teacher, don't you care if we drown?

(JESUS gets up and walks to the center of the boat. He's walking normally.)

DISCIPLE 3: Oh, the wind!

DISCIPLE 4: Oh, the rain!

DISCIPLE 5: Oh, the waves!

DISCIPLE 6: Oh, I think I'm gonna be sick!

JESUS: Oh, be quiet! Be still!

(Everything is calm. The DISCIPLES sit down. JESUS remains standing with arms folded, looking at the DISCIPLES.)

JESUS: Why are you so afraid? Do you still have no faith?

(The DISCIPLES are trembling, yet relieved.)

DISCIPLE 2: Aye, Sir. We were very afraid.

DISCIPLES 3–6: Thank You, Teacher.

(JESUS goes back to the stern and lies down.)

(DISCIPLE 2 raising an eyebrow and standing next to DISCIPLE 1 at his chair)

DISCIPLE 2: Most curious, captain.

DISCIPLE 1: Agreed. He's just as human as we are, but only God has that kind of authority over the wind and the waves. Curious, indeed.

(DISCIPLES 3-6 talk among themselves.)

Table Talk

What is most remarkable about this true story?

How are the actions of this man similar to the actions of Jesus on the cross? How are they different?

If you were on the tail of the plane that night and this mystery man handed you the rescue line, what might you think or say?

How might that affect your life?

Bible Study

The story of Jesus' crucifixion is a picture of a true hero. Jesus sacrificially chooses to die. He courageously suffers, dying for the sins of all humankind in order to rescue us from the consequences of sin. Read Luke 23:26–47.

1. In this story, how are Jesus' actions heroic?

2. Count the number of times the word "save" appears. Define the word "save." Why is it appropriate to use this word when talking about Jesus?

3. How is Jesus your personal Savior?

4. What attitude does Jesus have toward the crowd? the soldiers? the criminals?

5. What truth about Jesus does the criminal notice in 23:41?

6. Point out where the story proclaims the Law and the Gospel.

Family in Faith Journal

With your parent or mentor, write a prayer of thanksgiving to Jesus for His personal sacrifice for us. Record it in the Family in Faith Journal.

Fun for Review

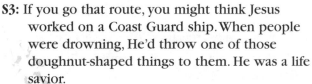

Characters: Teacher, 6 Students (S1 through S6)

Setting: Classroom. TEACHER is in front of the class, STUDENTS sit in their seats.

TEACHER: Class, today we're going to talk about Jesus' work.

S1: That's an easy subject. Jesus worked with wood and nails. He made things. You know, what's that called?

S2: A carpenter, brains!

S1: Oh, yeah. A carpenter.

S3: That was Jesus' dad, Joseph, who was the carpenter.

S1: But in those days, sons usually learned the work of their father. So He probably worked with wood and nails and stuff.

S2: Jesus worked as a teacher.

TEACHER: Tell me more about that.

S2: I think He probably taught people the most important lesson about working on a computer.

S1: What? Computer? They didn't have computers back then. They used something called typewriters.

S3: You've lost me.

S2: I figure Jesus was a computer teacher. He taught people the most important lesson: save your computer documents so they don't get lost. You've heard the news … "Jesus saves!"

S3: If you go that route, you might think Jesus worked on a Coast Guard ship. When people were drowning, He'd throw one of those doughnut-shaped things to them. He was a life savior.

S4: That's "lifesaver," dingy! Didn't He work as a doctor? He healed a bunch of people.

TEACHER: He did heal many people, but He wasn't a doctor.

S5: I thought Jesus must work in a cemetery because it seemed like that's where He really came to life. He loved His work there.

S6: My mom always says that Jesus knows the work of a mother because He was always making sacrifices for others.

TEACHER: Despite all your wild answers, your first guess was right, in a way. Jesus did work with wood and nails.

S1: See, I told you.

TEACHER: Jesus' greatest work was done when He was nailed to the cross—made of wood. He died so we could have forgiveness and salvation. He made the ultimate sacrifice on the cross.

S4: We were healed of our sins.

TEACHER: He was a great teacher, teaching us that the only way to heaven is by grace through faith in Him. Jesus was a lifesaver. He saved us from sin, death, and Satan. And on Easter morning He really did come to life! That's what Jesus' saving work is all about—that and so much more.

S2: Didn't I tell you in the first place? It's simple—Jesus saves!

Apostles' Creed, Third Article A

17

Table Talk

Jesus is our Savior and we thank Him for His sacrifice on the cross. But how important is the work of the Holy Spirit? Explain your answer.

When did the Holy Spirit first give you the benefits of Jesus' death and resurrection?

What other means of grace does the Holy Spirit use?

Bible Study

After Jesus dies, rises again, and ascends into heaven, the Holy Spirit continues Jesus' ministry through the apostles. Read Acts 2:32–47.

1. Where does Peter state that Jesus is a historical person? That He is the Christ?

2. Why were these elements necessary in Peter's preaching?

3. What effect does Peter's preaching have on the people?

4. According to the Third Article of the creed, who is behind this effect?

5. List as many words or phrases as you can in defining the chief work of the Holy Spirit.

6. Consider the fact that natural man is "spiritually blind, dead, and an enemy of God," and then review your list. Which of the words or phrases do you think best describes the fact that God, through the power of the Holy Spirit, creates faith in your heart?

7. Point out where the Bible story proclaims the Law and the Gospel.

Family in Faith Journal

Recall a time when you needed help and your parents helped you. Your parent or mentor should record this experience in the Family in Faith Journal.

Fun for Review

Props: Sign reading "LAW," sign reading "GOSPEL," sign reading "Right Path," sign reading "Wrong Path"

Characters: Wrong Crowd (2–3 people), Johnny, Holy Spirit, Narrator

Setting: Arrange the classroom so there are two distinct paths, one showing the "Right Path" and the other the "Wrong Path."

WRONG CROWD (1): *(In front of the Wrong Path sign)* Bummer you got caught drinking, man. Should have used a little mouthwash when you got home. Whadya do? Kiss your mommy goodnight?

(Other dudes laugh and make mock-kissing sounds.)

JOHNNY: No way! Just got busted, that's all. I told my parents I was sorry. They said, "No problem." Sort of.

WRONG CROWD (1): Well, listen! I heard about another party.

WRONG CROWD (2–3): Yeah—let's party! Another chance to ROCK!

WRONG CROWD (1): You with us tonight, Johnny-boy?

JOHNNY: Um, sure.

WRONG CROWD (2): Don't worry. If you do get caught—just give 'em that "I'm sorry" speech again. It worked the first time … *(Exits down Wrong Path)*

JOHNNY: Catch ya later, dudes!

HOLY SPIRIT: *(Spoken out of sight)* Hello, Johnny.

JOHNNY: Hello? Who are you?

HOLY SPIRIT: I am God. God the Holy Spirit, to be precise.

JOHNNY: God? Where are You? I can hear You, but I can't see You.

HOLY SPIRIT: I've been with you since your Baptism into Christ.

JOHNNY: You mean …

HOLY SPIRIT: Yes, I know about the party. It really hurts.

JOHNNY: Like I told my parents, I'm sorry. I know I shouldn't have done that. I know I shouldn't have gone with those guys.

HOLY SPIRIT: Are you truly sorry?

JOHNNY: Sure I am. By the way, God, if You need to help someone else, like later tonight, I'll be okay; go ahead …

HOLY SPIRIT: You're genuinely sorry for going against My will? *And* the will of your parents? Not to mention the will of the state—which says it's illegal for minors to drink?

JOHNNY: I said I was sorry, God! Isn't that enough? *(JOHNNY continues down the Wrong Path.)*

NARRATOR: Johnny continued down the wrong path. But the next day …

JOHNNY: *(Enters praying)* I'm sorry, Lord.

HOLY SPIRIT: *(Holding the Law sign up)* "It is the LORD your God you must follow, and Him you must revere. Keep His commands and obey Him; serve Him and hold fast to Him" (Deuteronomy 13:4).

JOHNNY: I know. I know.

HOLY SPIRIT: "Love the LORD your God with all your heart and with all your soul and with all your strength" (Deuteronomy 6:5).

JOHNNY: I know. I know. I do love You, Lord. But no matter how I try, I fail.

(The Law sign goes down; the Gospel sign goes up.)

HOLY SPIRIT: "But the Lord is faithful, and He will strengthen and protect you from the evil one" (2 Thessalonians 3:3).

JOHNNY: Thank You, Lord. And forgive me.

HOLY SPIRIT: "The LORD is gracious and compassionate, slow to anger and rich in love" (Psalm 145:8).

WRONG CROWD (1): *(Enters)* Johnny-boy! We're back! Let's go!

WRONG CROWD (2–3): Let's ROCK!

(JOHNNY starts to follow them again. And then stops suddenly. The WRONG CROWD keeps walking.)

JOHNNY: *(Talking to himself)* Wait! I said I was sorry! What am I doing?!

(Johnny turns around and goes down the Right Path.)

Bible Study

Because of persecution, the apostle John is exiled to the little island of Patmos. Jesus appears to Him and promises to take care of the church. Read Revelation 1:5b–20.

1. Describe in your own words the picture given in verse 7.

2. Since Alpha and Omega are the first and last letters of the Greek alphabet, what is Jesus saying about all of history and the role He plays in it?

3. What does the apostle John's experience in verse 9 teach you about the place of suffering in a Christian's life?

4. Ask your parent/mentor to share with you why it's comforting through good and bad times to know that Jesus is "the First and the Last … the Living One [who] was dead [but is now] alive forever and ever" (v. 17)?

5. What are the seven lampstands and where is Jesus in relation to them?

6. Despite the fact that even within our own church we may have arguments and disagreements, what comfort do we have as Christians?

7. Can you make the following statement: "If I should die tonight, because of God's grace in Jesus Christ received by my faith in Him, I know for sure I'd go to heaven."

8. Point out where the Bible story proclaims the Law and the Gospel.

Family in Faith Journal

With your parent or mentor, list names of family and friends who are not trusting Christ for salvation. In your Family in Faith Journal, compose a prayer that the Holy Spirit would lead them to repentance.

Fun for Review

Characters: Announcer, Survivors 1 (male), 2 (male), 3 (female), 4 (female), 5 (male) (Referred to in script as S1–S5)

Setting: Anywhere. Skit begins with S1 and S2 talking to each other; the other SURVIVORS enter when noted.

ANNOUNCER: Welcome to another episode of "Surviving!"—the hit show that follows the lives of people stranded in desperate places. From time to time one member is removed from the group. On our final episode, those surviving will win a precious crown of life. It is up to our group to figure out how they are going to survive. Let's see what the group is up to today.

S1: I don't know about you, but I'm starting to tire of all this.

S2: This is only day 4,732. We've been here 13 years. We could be here another 25,000 days or more, for all we know.

S1: But it seems like the same thing day after day. Same food. Same surroundings. Same people. Same everything. And we never know when we are going to be removed from the group. That's kind of nerve-racking.

S2: It could be worse. There are probably some people trying to figure out how many ways they can cook rats for supper and others eating kangaroo steaks every night. But we have a lot of stress too. Maybe we should form an alliance with some of the others so we'll know who is on our side.

S1: We could stick together and help each other.

S2: But we don't know whom we can trust.

S1: I don't know if I can even trust you! Maybe you're talking to me now because another alliance was formed and you're trying to figure out if I can be trusted!

S2: I'm on your side!

S1: I wonder about Survivor Number 3. She can be very nice, but then something happens and she seems completely different.

S2: I know what you mean. What about Number 5? I can't read him. He seems like a nice guy, but I'm always trying to figure out what's going on in his head.

S1: Number 4 seems like a real brain. She's always thinking, trying to figure things out.

S4: *(Enters)* Hi guys. I was just thinking.

S1: *(to S2)* What did I tell you?

S4: Actually, I was just reading. The book says, "Make every effort to keep the unity of the Spirit through the bond of peace" (Ephesians 4:3). I think the answer to surviving might be right in front of our eyes. I wonder if we are an alliance already, but we end up working against each other? *(Enter S3 and S5.)*

S3: We overheard what you were just saying. I was wondering the same thing. I think that we were chosen for a reason.

S5: What if the head of our group has chosen us to work together and to bring more people into this alliance, and here we are thinking too hard and not trusting each other?

S1: That's an interesting thought. *(To audience)* What do *you* think?

Morning and Evening Prayers

Table Talk

What role did daily prayer play in McCain's imprisonment?

How did the discovery that other prisoners were praying affect McCain?

Why might McCain continue to pray after he was set free?

Bible Study

Some of God's people being held in captivity in Babylon sought to stay there because they were enmeshed in the materialism of Babylon. Those who left were spiritually motivated to rebuild the temple and to reestablish Jerusalem. Read Ezra 3:1-6.

1. When did they make sacrifices?

2. What were God's people willing to do despite the fear of the people who surrounded them? See 3:3–6.

3. When we do God's work, who ridicules or frightens us?

4. In the Old Testament, God's people worshipped at the temple. What has taken the place of the temple and its sacrifices?

5. Prayer is not a "means of grace"—a way in which the Holy Spirit offers us the blessings of Christ and creates faith in us. If prayer does not give us God's grace, why then do we pray?

6. How do the blessings we receive during the worship service and family devotions help us with the fears we face?

7. Why make the sign of the holy cross before praying the Morning or Evening Prayers?

8. As you examine Luther's daily prayers, which words or statements are most meaningful to you?

9. Point out where the Bible story proclaims the Law and the Gospel.

Family in Faith Journal

Your parent or mentor will share how prayer has helped him or her to face life courageously and confidently. Your parent or mentor will record the story in the Family in Faith Journal.

Fun for Review

Characters: 1, 2, and 3

Setting: Performed in readers' theater style.

1: Pray without ceasing.

2: Pray without sleeping?

1: No. Pray without *ceasing*.

3: *Play* without ceasing?

1: No. *Pray* without *ceasing*.

2: No stopping?

3: Impossible.

1: All things are possible with God.

2: Can I pray while I sleep?

3: Can I pray while I play?

1: Commend yourself to God's care.

2: I commend my sleep to God's care.

3: I commend my play to God's care.

1: Commend your morning. Commend your evening.

2: Give your all to God.

3: Morning and evening.

1: Sleeping and waking.

2: Sleep in peace, trusting in God.

3: Sleep in peace, being a good manager of your bodies.

1: Play with joy.

2: Work with joy.

3: Who's Joy?

1: Joy comes with peace.

2: Peace and joy come in commending your all to God.

1: Morning and evening.

3: Waking and sleeping.

2: Pray continually.

1: That's what I say.

3: That's what God says.

2: That's what Paul says.

3: 1 Thessalonians 5:17.

1: Pray with thanksgiving.

2: Pray for forgiveness.

3: Pray for protection.

1: Pray to the Father through Jesus Christ.

2: Play in His name.

3: Thankfully play.

1: Play, protected by angels.

2: Live forgiven.

3: Pray without ceasing.

1: In the name of the Father.

2: In the name of the Son.

3. In the name of the Holy Spirit.

1: Amen.

2: Amen.

3: So be it!

Lord's Prayer, Introduction and Conclusion

Bible Study

When sinners gather to hear Jesus teach, the Pharisees feel offended. Then Jesus tells a parable. Read Luke 15:11–24.

1. What was Jesus' main point of telling the story of the prodigal son?

2. Describe a time when you resembled each of these characters in one way or another: (a) the Prodigal Son, (b) the father.

3. Read verse 21. Does the son really have faith in his father's forgiveness?

4. Read aloud verse 20. Does the prodigal son say anything to his father before the father embraces him? What assurance do you receive from that thought?

5. How did the son come to believe the father would forgive him? See Luke 15:22.

6. What boldness does this story give us when it comes to approaching God in prayer, even when we've been disobedient and far away from Him?

7. As we spend time in prayer, praying according to God's Word, how might God change us?

8. Point out where the story proclaims the Law and the Gospel.

Family in Faith Journal

List five words that describe a father and discuss them with your parent or mentor. How do they apply to the heavenly Father? Record the discussion in the Family in Faith Journal.

Fun for Review

Props: Play food and cooking utensils, apron (a chef's hat would be nice), trays and napkins—items a waiter may use

Characters: Pierre, the Head Chef (give it your best French accent!); Lost Son; Servants (2–3); Forgiving Father

Setting: The back kitchen

(SERVANTS are gathered around PIERRE. He speaks with nervous excitement.)

PIERRE: You should have seen it! Day after day, Monsieur was waiting at the end of the driveway. It was truly a sad sight to behold. Ah, the poor old man. He would scan the horizon, until one afternoon, voila! He sees his son coming in the distance! *(Clapping hands for orders)* And now, here we are. We are to throw a party! And a party it will be!

FORGIVING FATHER: *(Rushes in)* Okay! Okay! Pierre? Make everything right! I want the best fattened calf we've got. I want it to be a great feast! For this son of mine was dead and is alive again; he was lost and is found! LET'S CELEBRATE! *(Exits)*

PIERRE: We have work to do! You! Get the best, largest calf we have! And you! Come here and grate this parmesan cheese! Snap to it, rapidement! Now we need someone to help set the table … you! Come here!

LOST SON: *(Turns and points to himself)* Me, sir?

PIERRE: Ahhhhh! What are you doing here? Does your father know you're here? You don't belong here! This place is for the servants. You're not a servant. You're a son! You are an heir of this house!

LOST SON: But I don't deserve to be a son. I don't even deserve to be at the table. Pierre, let me work back here with you! I will be a good servant. I promise!

PIERRE: Ahhhhh! No! No, you can't! Did you not hear what your pa-pa has told you? You were lost! And now? You are found!

LOST SON: Yes, but I don't deserve what my father has said. Let me work here for a while—a few weeks, maybe. Then I can say I actually earned my way back.

PIERRE: Ahhhhh, contraire! No! I will not have it! This is not something for you to earn. It is by the grace of your father that he has welcomed you back to the house!

FORGIVING FATHER: My son! My son! What are you doing in here? You should be out there with the guests. You are not a slave; you are my dear son.

SERVANTS (1–3): Slaves?

PIERRE: Quiet, you! I'll explain later. Back to work!

LOST SON: I've embarrassed you, Dad. I've embarrassed the family name. Now I deserve nothing but the crumbs that fall from the kitchen counter.

FORGIVING FATHER: Yes, you are right.

LOST SON: I am?

PIERRE: Ahhhhh! No worry! We will prepare the best parmesan crumbs in the world!

FORGIVING FATHER: Pierre, please. Just make the feast. *(PIERRE goes to work with SERVANTS.)* Son, you do not deserve even the title of slave. But I forgive you. And by this forgiveness you are made whole again and are once again an heir to this estate. Now come, let us go to the banquet table.

(FORGIVING FATHER and LOST SON embrace, then exit.)

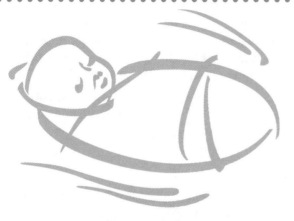

Bible Study

Nicodemus, a great religious and political leader, sneaks in to visit Jesus at night. Jesus tells him about the kingdom of God. Read John 3:1–8.

1. The Greek phrase "born again" can mean being "born from above." In what way is our rebirth truly something that takes place from "above" (see also 1 Corinthians 2:14)?

2. What response did Nicodemus have when Jesus said one must be born again to enter the kingdom of God?

3. What does Jesus describe when He refers to "water and the Spirit"?

4. Through water and the Holy Spirit, God makes us holy. Name specific ways you keep God's name holy.

5. Are there some family members or friends at school who have not entered the "kingdom of God"? If so, include these people in your prayers, asking that God would use you and others to bring God's kingdom to them.

6. Point out where the Bible story proclaims the Law and the Gospel.

Family in Faith Journal

Your parent or mentor will complete the following statement: "All children are special. But I especially thank God for my child because … ." Write the response in the Family in Faith Journal.

Fun for Review

Props: 2 chairs

Characters: Rick, a TV show host; Nic(odemus)

Setting: Television-program set. RICK and NIC are sitting.

RICK: Hello! I'm Rick, your host tonight. We have a special guest on the show. Please welcome Nic at Night to our "Nic at Night" show! Whoa, that's cool. You have the same name as our show. That's so cool! Well, Nic, why don't you start by telling us about yourself?

NIC: Thank you for having me. Nic is short for Nicodemus. I used to be a Pharisee, a member of the Jewish ruling council in Jerusalem.

RICK: Fascinating, Nic, simply fascinating.

NIC: I received the rest of my nickname because I went to talk to Jesus one night. I wasn't brave enough to be seen with Him during the day. That's why people call me Nic at Night—get it?

RICK: I think so, Nic.

NIC: But all that has changed for me now. I guess I should be called "Nic in the Light"!

RICK: How were you changed?

NIC: It's a matter of who and what changed me, first of all.

RICK: Who? What? When? Where? Take a stab at them all, Nic!

NIC: The "who" is Jesus Christ. He's the one I went to talk to and He's the one who changed me. He told me that no one can see the kingdom of God unless he is born again.

RICK: I bet that about floored you, Nic.

NIC: Just about, Rick. I didn't understand everything He was telling me at the time, but now I fully understand because He changed me through His Word and through Baptism.

RICK: Words can change people, Nic at Night who's now in the light, right?

NIC: I am walking in the light of Jesus Christ. His Word changed my life, Rick. The Holy Spirit changes people. He brings them forgiveness. He places His holy name on them. He gives them eternal life. He brings them out of the darkness of sin into His perfect light.

RICK: So the sin is like darkness. And His Holy Spirit uses God's Word and Baptism to bring people into His light? Is that right, Nic?

NIC: That's right, Rick.

RICK: Wow.

NIC: Wow, indeed! And now instead of being in the kingdom of the Pharisees I am part of the kingdom of God! I live in His light.

RICK: So you're not scared to talk about Jesus Christ in public anymore.

NIC: No more wimping out and meeting Jesus in the dark. We walk together in His light. I am not ashamed of Jesus or His holy name or His perfect light and life.

RICK: You are really pumped about this Jesus, aren't you, Nic?

NIC: I am, Rick. His kingdom has come to me. His name is holy to me. And I have been changed by the Holy Spirit's power, working through God's Word.

RICK: It sounds like no more "Nic at Night" for you, huh?

NIC: Forget sneaking around at night. I want to bring everyone the light of Jesus. I'm Nic in the Light! Nic in the Light! Nic in the Light!

Table Talk

What might Rosa's neighbors have said about God's will when Rosa had only $12.85 left to run her school?

Before Rosa had prayed and sought help for the school, could she have guessed what God's will was? Explain your answer.

If circumstances can't tell us God's will, where can we learn God's will?

What is the most important thing God wants for each of us?

Bible Study

Joseph's brothers scheme to get rid of him. When a caravan of merchantmen comes along, they sell Joseph and tell their father that Joseph has been brutally killed by an animal. Years later, they discover he is still alive when they come to Egypt for food because of a famine. Read Genesis 45:1–7.

1. Despite the brother's plans, God had a different plan. What was God's plan according to Joseph? See verses 5–7.

2. Have you ever argued over God's will? What was it over? Who won the argument?

3. How do you think Joseph's brothers felt after discovering that God's will was far different from theirs?

4. Name some of the things that we know are God's will.

5. Identify times when you've found it difficult to do God's will. What forces hindered you from doing it?

6. What does the forgiveness that Joseph offers to his brothers teach us about God's will?

7. How vital is forgiveness to the life of a Christian?

8. Point out where the story proclaims the Law and the Gospel.

Family in Faith Journal

Your parent or mentor will describe a time when he or she was not sure what God's will was for their lives. Ask how things were resolved and record the story in the Family in Faith Journal.

Fun for Review

Prop: Kleenex

Characters: Joseph, Rueben, Benjamin, Zebulun, Simeon, Levi, Judah, Issachar

Setting: Genesis 45:15—at the palace. Everyone is blowing his nose, tearful yet happy.

JOSEPH: Brothers! Brothers! Listen. It is good to be here with you. After Dan, Naphtali, Gad, and Asher return with our father, we will have a great celebration! In the meantime, let's talk about what happened. Isn't this so cool?

RUEBEN: What's cool?

JOSEPH: How I got here!

BENJAMIN: *(Still sobbing)* You mean you're not mad at us?

ALL BROTHERS: BENJAMIN!

JOSEPH: No. I am not. In fact, I am amazed at the way our God works. When you guys sold me into slavery, I was scared. Then it became apparent that God was at work here. If you hadn't been jealous of me, this would have never happened! Isn't that great?

RUEBEN: No. I mean, we're glad you're okay, Joseph. But we never should have faked your death. We never should have been jealous of Dad's love for you.

ZEBULUN: *(Looking at BENJAMIN)* Benny, is that really Joseph?

BENJAMIN: *(Starting to cry louder)* Yes. Yes, it is!

ZEBULUN: Wow!

JOSEPH: I know you shouldn't have, Rueben. But isn't it amazing how God can use our sinful acts to bring about blessings? It was God's will. This was God's will! By the way, what did you do with my coat?

SIMEON: Coat?

LEVI: Um, well, you see …

JUDAH: It was God's will that we tear it …

ISSACHAR: And it was God's will that we put animal blood on it …

RUEBEN: And then, well, it was His will that we throw it away.

SIMEON: It looked pretty yucky.

BENJAMIN: Ohhh, the coat!

ZEBULUN: Joseph? You okay?

JOSEPH: You threw it away! I wouldn't call what you did with my coat "God's will." That's stretching it a bit, bros. Oh well, it doesn't really matter. That coat is a distant memory. What's important now is that there's a deliverance!

RUEBEN: You're right! Dad will be so glad!

SIMEON: I'm actually looking forward to Goshen.

ISSACHAR: It's time to leave the ranch!

LEVI: Yee haw!

Lord's Prayer, Fourth Petition

Table Talk

Does hardship mean that God has abandoned us? Explain your answer.

What in Miriam's experience gave her confidence in God's care?

Why pray for daily bread if you have enough to eat?

Bible Study

Paul is confronted in Athens with a city full of idols and people who philosophize about life and death. Paul presents the people with new hope through the preaching of the Gospel. Read Acts 17:16–31.

1. How does verse 21 describe many people today in their search for spirituality?

2. How does Paul describe God as a personal Creator and Designer of all things?

3. What comfort do you receive from knowing that God has not left things to happen by chance?

4. According to Paul, where do all good things come from?

5. If God owns everything, including the power of life and death, what would God have you do with your life?

6. If God gives us daily bread without our asking, why do some people worry about not having enough?

7. Can you identify someone who does not have the "daily bread" he/she needs to survive? Name some things you and your mentor might do to help this person.

8. Point out where the Bible story proclaims the Law and the Gospel.

9. What does Christ provide for you that is even more precious than daily bread?

Family in Faith Journal

Describe to your parent or mentor a memorable Thanksgiving Day meal. He or she should record this memory in the Family in Faith Journal.

Fun for Review

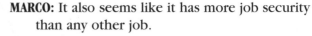

Characters: Marco, Katerina

KATERINA: Hi, Marco! What did you think about that special presentation on future vocations?

MARCO: I was disappointed at first because I thought it was about future **vacations**!

KATERINA: *(Laughing)* I guess you were surprised to find us discussing future jobs instead of travel plans to the mountains or beach! But did you find the presentation helpful?

MARCO: It made me think. I've thought about a lot of different jobs I might work at someday.

KATERINA: Like what?

MARCO: A couple of years ago I wanted to be an airplane pilot. Then I realized pilots don't have much employment security since their jobs are always up in the air.

KATERINA: Very funny! That's kind of a *plane* job anyway!

MARCO: Then I thought about being a baseball player, but that might drive me *batty*.

KATERINA: I figured you would have *a ball* in that profession.

MARCO: How about you, Katerina? You enjoy basketball.

KATERINA: I figure at my height I won't have *a shot* at being a professional woman's basketball player.

MARCO: I agree. But after today's seminar, I'm thinking about being a bread delivery person.

KATERINA: What made you think about that job?

MARCO: Think about it. There's a lot of *loafing* around! I wouldn't loaf around, of course, because I'd want to do a good job for my employer, who will be paying me a lot of *dough* for my work!

KATERINA: Those are, ummm, interesting thoughts!

MARCO: It also seems like it has more job security than any other job.

KATERINA: Why do you say that?

MARCO: Everyone wants bread. Everyone wants bread every day. There must be a great need for bread delivery people.

KATERINA: I guess people eat a lot of bread.

MARCO: Just think about it. Don't you think that all over the world "The Lord's Prayer" must be prayed a million times a day?

KATERINA: I guess. But now you're confusing me.

MARCO: Every time "The Lord's Prayer" is prayed by someone, they pray, "Give us this day our daily bread." People want bread so much that they're praying for it. The world needs people to deliver that bread. And that will be me.

KATERINA: *(Laughing)* I have a funny feeling you're not joking this time.

MARCO: It's nothing to joke about.

KATERINA: No, it isn't. But I need to explain something to you. When people are praying, "Give us this day our daily bread," they aren't asking for wheat, white, or rye.

MARCO: Really?

KATERINA: Really! The phrase "daily bread" means anything that supports our daily life.

MARCO: Well, if that is true, I guess the job of delivering "daily bread" is already taken.

KATERINA: What do you mean?

MARCO: The only true "daily bread deliverer" is God. He's the one who gives us all that we need.

KATERINA: He certainly does deliver! But God also uses His people to bring others what they need. So whatever job you end up having, there will be part of a "daily bread delivery person" in you!

MARCO: I like that thought, Kat! Since that is the case, maybe I'll just do what my dad does for a living. He repairs shoes. He's always said that he's in the business of saving *soles*!

Blessing and Thanksgiving

24

Table Talk

After so much suffering, how could Pastor Rinckart write a hymn of thanks to God?

Why might God permit such suffering?

Why is it appropriate to pray the Lord's Prayer whenever we offer blessings for our food or return thanks?

3. Re-create that scene today in a large metropolitan city. Suppose there were many people with Jesus and He started to distribute bread and fish to eat. How do you think most people would react?

4. If you were one of the five thousand, what would your reaction be?

5. Recall Psalm 23:1. How does the psalmist summarize the meaning of Mark 6:42?

Bible Study

Jesus leaves His home town, where many people doubt He is the Christ. Then King Herod kills Jesus' cousin, John the Baptist. Jesus leads His disciples to a quiet place for rest. Read Mark 6:30–44.

1. What does Jesus do before this meal?

6. As you review your blessings, for what are you led to give thanks to God?

7. Point out where the Bible story proclaims the Law and the Gospel.

2. Though they had only five loaves of bread and two fish, what did Jesus do? See verse 41.

Family in Faith Journal

Your parent or mentors will ask you what table prayers you typically use. Record these in the Family in Faith Journal.

Fun for Review

Prop: Paper sack (for lunch)

Characters: Zach, Sauley

Setting: The place where Jesus fed the 5,000

ZACH: There are a lot of people here.

SAULEY: Everyone wants to hear Jesus speak.

ZACH: I saw him heal a man who was deaf.

SAULEY: That's unheard of.

ZACH: Really, I saw it.

SAULEY: I watched Him give a man back his sight. The man believed Jesus could heal him.

ZACH: That's what I call blind faith!

SAULEY: He's a great teacher, too.

ZACH: It's hard to hear Him with so many people.

SAULEY: I wish someone would invent woofers and tweeters so we could hear better.

ZACH: I have a dog that woofs and a bird that tweets. How will they help?

SAULEY: Never mind.

ZACH: I'm starting to get hungry.

SAULEY: My mom packed some food.

ZACH: Whatcha got?

SAULEY: I haven't checked yet. I hope it's either peanut butter and matzo ball sandwiches or kosher pickles. *(Looks in bag)* Aw, shucks.

ZACH: Shucks? She packed some shucks?

SAULEY: No, just a couple of fish and five loaves of bread.

ZACH: Be quiet … what is that follower of Jesus asking?

(Pause while ZACH and SAULEY pretend to listen.)

SAULEY: He's asking if anyone has food to share.

ZACH: Offer your sack lunch.

SAULEY: I only have a little. My mom would be embarrassed for not packing enough for everyone!

ZACH: The disciple of Jesus is coming over here. I think he saw that you had food.

SAULEY: *(Looking up and speaking to disciple)* Ummm, certainly you can have my food, but it isn't much. Yes, I know the Master has need of it. Gladly I will give it to you.

ZACH: Sauley, he's giving it to Jesus. No one else had any food to share.

SAULEY: I hope my mom de-boned the fish. I don't want Jesus or His disciples to choke on my mom's fish. Oh, the guilt she'd live with if that happened.

ZACH: Listen, Jesus is blessing the food—your food. The fish and the bread.

SAULEY: He wants us to get into groups to eat. *(Looking around)* How is He going to feed this huge group? There must be some 5,000 men here, and that's not counting women and children.

ZACH: Jesus is holding up your food. He's giving thanks for it. Sauley, you're going to be famous. You would be on all the evening newscasts, if someone had invented television.

SAULEY: They are passing the food around. It looks like there's enough for everyone.

ZACH: It's a miracle. How did He do that?

SAULEY: He blessed the food and gave thanks. That's all I saw and heard.

ZACH: This Jesus is a miracle worker who knows what people need and answers them.

SAULEY: I bet my mom's food tastes even better because it was blessed by Jesus and because He gave thanks for it.

Lord's Prayer, Fifth Petition 25

***

25

Table Talk

What made it possible for these two boys to sit together peacefully in class?

Close your eyes and recall the last person you fought or argued with. In view of this story, what would you like to say to that person?

Recall the worst thing that has ever happened to you. Have you forgiven the person or persons involved? Why or why not?

***

Bible Study

Jesus teaches His disciples to talk to the people who offend them. Peter asks how often he should forgive others. Jesus answers with a parable. Read Matthew 18:23–35.

1. As followers of Jesus, what are we called on to do? See 18:33.

2. What is the worst thing that could happen if you forgave someone who wasn't truly sorry? What's the best thing that could happen?

3. In the creed we have learned that God forgives us freely through Christ. Does verse 35 mean that unless we forgive one another we may lose God's forgiveness?

4. What do you deserve because of your sin?

5. What is so amazing about God's gracious forgiveness?

6. Point out where the Bible story proclaims the Law and the Gospel.

Family in Faith Journal

Your parent or mentor will describe a time he or she struggled to forgive someone. Talk about God's forgiveness for all sins through Christ. Do not necessarily record this in the Family in Faith Journal!

Fun for Review

Props: 2 pretend microphones

Characters: Larry, the announcer; John Dibbs, a reporter; Kay Karowitz, another reporter; Mrs. Chen Selikah, the victim's mother; Ricky Riqqab, the perpetrator; Andy Dexter, someone from the public; a couple of police officers

Setting: A city street and the county jail

ANNOUNCER: We interrupt this program for this Special Report with John Dibbs. John, what do we know?

DIBBS: A terrible crime was committed in Midtown. Police won't let us get any closer, and that's just as well. It looks pretty blucky.

ANNOUNCER: Excuse me, John?

DIBBS: Awful, Larry. It looks awful. Apparently one man beat another man silly because he owed him money. And here's the really blucky part: we heard the victim shouting, "Have mercy! Have mercy!" And, by the looks of things, the attacker did not. Larry?

ANNOUNCER: I understand you have an eyewitness to this blucky event. John?

DIBBS: Larry, Mr. Andy Dexter says he knows what happened. Want to tell us what you know?

DEXTER: *(Excitedly)* OH MAN! THIS IS HORRIBLE! I CAN'T BELIEVE IT …

ANNOUNCER: John! John! Calm that man down!

DIBBS: Sir! Sir! *(Pause)* Chill.

DEXTER: Sorry! Sorry! I just can't believe it. Ricky Riqqab, that notorious, evil embezzler—you know, the one that the Governor pardoned last week?

DIBBS: Yes.

DEXTER: Well, I saw him go up to a so-called friend of his AND BEAT THAT MAN SILLY!

ANNOUNCER: Silly? This isn't funny!

DIBBS: Remember, it's an expression, Larry. And what happened next, sir?

DEXTER: It was awful! Simply awful! I could never forgive that evil Riqqab for what he did! The whole thing makes me sick. It's downright blucky, if you ask me.

DIBBS: There you have it, Larry. A truly blucky tragedy here in Midtown.

ANNOUNCER: Thank you, John. Let's go live now to reporter Kay Karowitz, who has word from the county jail. Okay, Kay, take it away!

KAROWITZ: This is scary, Larry. According to police, we're going to talk to the allegedly notorious and evil perpetrator, Richard Riqqab. And here he is now!

(POLICE bring RIQQAB up to KAROWITZ, handcuffed.)

KAROWITZ: Sir, you've been charged with beating a man silly! Did you indeed beat the man silly in Midtown today?

RIQQAB: I have no comment. But if I *did* have a comment, I would most likely say that he deserved it!

KAROWITZ: So you did it?

RIQQAB: If I were talking, I would say that THE LITTLE SQUIRT OWED ME MONEY! *(RIQQAB is taken away.)*

KAROWITZ: Wait! I see the mother of the victim. Excuse me, ma'am? Can we talk to you for a moment?

SELIKAH: Yes?

KAROWITZ: What is your name? Was it your son? Are you here to confront the alleged perpetrator? Do you like squash? Do you have the time? How is your son? And what is your favorite color?

SELIKAH: *(Slight pause after each answer, thinking)* Mrs. Chen Selikah. Yes … Yes … No … It's *(gives the time)* … Fine … And yellow!

ANNOUNCER: Ask if she is related to Tom Selleck.

KAROWITZ: No, Larry. Where is your son, Ma'am?

SELIKAH: He's in the hospital, but recovering well. He wanted me to come down here and tell Ricky Riqqab that my son forgives him.

KAROWITZ: WHAT?

ANNOUNCER: WHAT?

DIBBS: WHAT?

SELIKAH: *(Puzzled)* Well, yes.

KAROWITZ: Will your son still pay back the money he *allegedly* owes this *alleged* perpetrator?

SELIKAH: Of course he will. *(Walks away)*

KAROWITZ: There you have it, Larry. Truly amazing!

ANNOUNCER: I can't believe it!

Bible Study

Joseph's brothers sell him as a slave into Egypt. An Egyptian ruler named Potiphar buys Joseph and eventually trusts him with running his household. Read Genesis 39:1–23.

1. Considering all the things that happened to Joseph—his family's rejection, a plot to have him killed, being sold into slavery—would you have blamed him had he simply given up and surrendered to despair? Why?

2. What might have happened to Joseph if he gave in to this temptation?

3. What temptations do you face daily? How are you able to resist them? Or don't you?

4. When Luther writes, "God tempts no one," what misunderstanding of the Sixth Petition is he trying to clear up?

5. Have you ever been tempted in the following ways? If so, describe those times.
"Don't worry, everyone is doing it."

"It doesn't matter what you believe as long as you really believe it."

"Every religion is the same. Each one just has a little different way to heaven."

"Why do you even try ... you'll never make it."

"If God didn't want you to have sex, He wouldn't have created you with the desire."

6. Read 2 Timothy 4:18. What does God promise for you in this passage?

7. How does Joseph remind you of Jesus?

8. Point out where the Bible story proclaims the Law and the Gospel.

Family in Faith Journal

You will be paired with another student. Ask each other, "Are you more likely to give into temptation when you are with your peers or when alone?" Record these thoughts in the Family in Faith Journal.

Fun for Review

Characters: Monique, Erick, Monique's Thoughts, Erick's Thoughts, Teacher

Setting: School classroom. ERICK and MONIQUE are seated facing the group, taking a test. There are two chairs directly behind theirs, facing the opposite direction. Their THOUGHTS will speak from these chairs.

(Throughout the sketch ERICK continually tries to sneak a peak at MONIQUE's test. Both students should react as their THOUGHTS speak.)

ERICK'S THOUGHTS: I knew I should have studied more for this test. Monique is so smart, she probably thinks this is easy.

MONIQUE'S THOUGHTS: Wow, this is easy!

ERICK'S THOUGHTS: She's flying through those answers. I'm not even sure I spelled my name right.

MONIQUE'S THOUGHTS: This one is obviously false. That one is true.

ERICK'S THOUGHTS: I wonder if she'd notice if I took a quick peek at her answers.

MONIQUE'S THOUGHTS: This one is … hey, is Erick trying to peek at my answers?

ERICK'S THOUGHTS: Let's see, it's the true-false section. I wish I had better odds than 50–50! She writes like a girl. I can't tell if that's a "T" or an "F."

MONIQUE'S THOUGHTS: Should I let him cheat, or should I just glare at him? He's really nice, and I know he's busy with sports. Maybe I should let him see my answers.

ERICK'S THOUGHTS: I think she put "True" for the first one. Wait! I can't do this. *(Pause)* I shouldn't do this. *(Pause)* I could do this! *(Pause)* I wouldn't cheat. Would I?

MONIQUE'S THOUGHTS: What am I thinking? I worked hard to get a good grade. Besides, it's not right to let him cheat.

ERICK'S THOUGHTS: I wish our chairs weren't so close together. This is the teacher's fault. He wants to test us to see if we'll cheat.

MONIQUE'S THOUGHTS: I guess I could let him see an answer or two. He is kind of cute.

ERICK'S THOUGHTS: I wonder if she thinks I'm cute. Maybe that will be in my favor.

MONIQUE'S THOUGHTS: No! Stop it! Concentrate on your test. You're wasting time. Get back to work.

ERICK'S THOUGHTS: I'm gonna flunk this test.

MONIQUE'S THOUGHTS: I'm going to ace this test.

ERICK'S THOUGHTS: I will not cheat. I will not cheat. I will get an "F."

MONIQUE'S THOUGHTS: This essay is an easy one.

ERICK'S THOUGHTS: What's up with this essay?

(Pause)

TEACHER: Time is up. Pass your papers forward. I tried something different for this test. I mixed up the test questions so no two people sitting next to each other would be able to cheat, or if you did, you probably marked the wrong answer! I thought that might help keep you from the temptation to cheat on future tests.

ERICK'S THOUGHTS: Oh, isn't he the clever one!

MONIQUE'S THOUGHTS: Since Erick seemed to struggle on this test, maybe I will offer to help him study for the next test.

TEACHER: It's time for religion class. Everyone take out your Bibles and turn to Genesis 39. We're going to learn about someone else who was tested.

Baptism and Its Benefits

Bible Study

Jesus' last recorded words in Matthew echo the command He gives to each and every one of us—to make disciples. In His command He tells us how to specifically do it. Read Matthew 28:16–20.

1. According to Jesus, what two actions make disciples? See 28:19–20.

2. In what way are our parents following these instructions by placing us in confirmation classes?

3. When Jesus says, "all nations," what age groups does that include for Baptism?

4. If people in other countries have their own religions, why would Jesus tell His followers to make disciples of all nations?

5. Talk about a Baptism you've seen in church. What happened? Who gave the church the right to baptize?

6. Was the Baptism that of an infant? Who said he/she even wanted to be baptized?

7. A Baptist friend in school says your religion is wrong because you believe that infants should be baptized. How would you explain or defend the practice of your church?

8. Point out where the story proclaims the Law and the Gospel.

Family in Faith Journal

Your parent or mentor will describe a time when he or she faced death, injury, or destruction. How did they get through it? How did God help? Record the events in the Family in Faith Journal.

Fun for Review

Characters: Suzy, Billy, Bobby, Amy

Setting: Outside of class talking about Baptism

SUZY: I still can't believe your parents didn't have you baptized when you were a baby, Billy.

BILLY: They just didn't, okay?

BOBBY: Hey, that's okay. You're getting baptized before Confirmation Day, and I think that's great!

AMY: I think it makes more sense to wait until you're older anyway.

BOBBY: What?

SUZY: You do?

AMY: Sure. Billy will be able to remember his Baptism Day. Right? Can any of you remember the day you were baptized?

BOBBY: I was three weeks old. If I could remember, that would be a little scary.

SUZY: I can't remember, but I've seen pictures!

AMY: My mom said I threw up all over the pastor's robe. I certainly don't remember that, and it's just as well. Now, if I had been older, then that wouldn't have happened, right?

BOBBY: That's not the point, Amy. You were baptized as an infant, I was, and Suzy was because our parents were following Christ's command to go and baptize all nations. That includes babies, children, and adults.

AMY: Yeah, but I still think it makes sense to wait, so the person being baptized can really appreciate their Baptism.

BOBBY: I do appreciate my Baptism, *thank you*.

SUZY: Are you looking forward to Sunday, Billy?

BILLY: Yeah, sort of.

BOBBY: Sort of? This is going to be awesome!

AMY: There, you see! It's going to be awesome—and even more awesome because Billy will be able to remember its awesomeness. Right, Billy-boy?

BILLY: I suppose.

BOBBY: I think you're mixing up what is really important here. If you remember your Baptism because you were older, wonderful. But what really matters is that God remembers! And He does. Baptism is something God is doing for you, not the other way around.

AMY: Yeah, but a baby can't recognize that this is something God is doing. So how can a baby appreciate it?

SUZY: Oooo, good question, *Aim*. Answer that one, Robert!

BOBBY: Let me put it this way. When a baby is born, do you think that baby recognizes her daddy?

AMY: No. She's just an infant.

BOBBY: Exactly. But just because the baby doesn't recognize her daddy, does that make him any less her daddy?

AMY: I guess not.

BOBBY: Of course it doesn't! Parents don't wait until their children can call them by name before they declare themselves to be the parents!

BILLY: What's your point, *Pastor* Bob?

BOBBY: Very funny. My point is this: the benefits of Baptism come from God—His Word connected with the water! Through Baptism God gives the gift of faith to the child. It is a gift, not a reward for being someone special or smart or whatever. Baptism is "grace given," not a "wage earned"!

SUZY: So, Billy, I guess you're not so special after all. See? Told you so.

BILLY: Ha-ha, Suze. So does this mean that I'm not God's child until I get baptized? Does this mean I don't have His grace until Sunday?

How Baptism Works

Table Talk

How does Baptism take us out of the devil's kingdom and bring us into God's kingdom?

Are all people God's children by birth? Explain.

Bible Study

Acts 2 gives us a picture of the newborn church, how it was formed and what it looked like once it came into existence. Those who were baptized looked and acted totally differently than they did before their conversion. Read Acts 2:22–47.

1. When Peter gives his sermon, what themes does he focus on?

2. What new promise does Peter proclaim in verses 38–39?

3. How does God fulfill this promise to His people?

4. Once baptized, what was extraordinary about the way the believers lived? See Acts 2:42–47.

5. Name someone in your life who truly lives out his/her Christian faith. What does he/she do that makes him/her extraordinary?

6. According to Mark 16:16, what condemns a person (see *LSCE*, p. 22)?

7. If you are baptized, what comfort or encouragement does that provide for you?

8. Point out where the story proclaims the Law and the Gospel.

Family in Faith Journal

From your parents or church records, learn your baptismal date and sponsors. Record them in the Family in Faith Journal.

Fun for Review

Prop: Notebook

Characters: Tommy, Mom

Setting: Their home

MOM: So how was school today?

TOMMY: Fine.

MOM: That's what you always say. Tell me something you learned today.

TOMMY: I dunno. I learned math in math class and English in English class.

MOM: What did you learn in confirmation class today? And don't say, "I learned confirmation in confirmation class." That doesn't work.

TOMMY: Oh, I did learn something cool today. I found out a way to tell which adults are baptized and which aren't just by looking at them.

MOM: What? You're telling me that you can tell who is baptized by looking at them?

TOMMY: Yep. Like Mr. Parlidge. I can tell he's not baptized.

MOM: You're kidding. I'm sure he is.

TOMMY: Not according to what I learned in class today.

MOM: I can't believe Pastor would tell you that.

TOMMY: He didn't mention Mr. Parlidge by name, but I know he isn't baptized because of what Pastor taught us today about Baptism.

MOM: I'm confused.

TOMMY: I don't think Mr. Ewing, Mr. Rodriguez, or even Mrs. Sardis are baptized!

MOM: Now come on. Mr. Ewing is one of the elders at church. He's baptized. Mr. Rodriguez teaches the adult Bible class. He even taught a class on Baptism. You're just trying to get me to stop asking you what you learned in school every day.

TOMMY: I'm telling the truth, Mom.

MOM: Okay, tell me exactly what you talked about today in confirmation class. What did Pastor teach you?

TOMMY: He told us that our hair is made through Baptism.

MOM: What?

TOMMY: I thought about the last baby I saw baptized. She didn't have any hair, but I noticed last week in church her hair was growing.

MOM: And what about Mr. Parlidge, Mr. Ewing, Mr. Rodriguez, and Mrs. Sardis?

TOMMY: Haven't you noticed they're all bald?

MOM: Mrs. Sardis isn't bald!

TOMMY: Well, she's awfully close to bald! Mr. Sardis has more hair than she does!

MOM: This still doesn't make sense. Now you said Pastor told you that our hair is made through Baptism?

TOMMY: I'm sure he did. At least I'm pretty sure. Look, here are my notes. *(Hands notebook to MOM)*

MOM *(Reading notes)* You wrote down, "We are made hairs through Baptism." *(Starts to laugh)* Tommy! Pastor said, "We are made **heirs**, not **hairs** through Baptism"!

TOMMY: Oops. What does heirs mean?

MOM: An heir is someone who gets an inheritance. Through our Baptism we are heirs of forgiveness, salvation, and all of God's incredible gifts. That's all part of our inheritance because we are children of God through Baptism.

TOMMY: I guess that makes a lot of difference.

MOM: I think you better listen more closely in class. And ask questions if you don't understand!

TOMMY: I think so too!

MOM: It's time for bed. Go take your shower first … and wash your hair, you heir of salvation through Baptism!

TOMMY: Very funny, Mom!

Table Talk

Why was Louis' Baptism so important to him?

In the lesson on daily prayers Luther encouraged us to make the sign of the cross each day. How does that practice fit with this part of the catechism on Baptism?

Bible Study

After a group of Pharisees ask Jesus about the coming of the kingdom of God, He tells a series of parables about daily Christian life. Read Luke 18:9–14.

1. Though both men came to the temple, what was the problem with the Pharisee?

2. If you had been a Pharisee listening to this parable, how do you think you'd have felt about what Jesus said? Convicted? Angry? Uneasy?

3. What made the tax collector's confession acceptable before God? See also Psalm 51:16–17.

4. Put Luke 18:14 into your own words.

5. Define the words "righteousness" and "justified."

6. Complete the following sentence: Because of Baptism, I know I am …

7. How do you continue to drown the Old Adam within?

8. What's the biggest change in you because of Jesus?

9. Point out where the story proclaims the Law and the Gospel.

Family in Faith Journal

Your parent or mentor will describe a time when he or she was tempted to give up. Discuss the hope and strength provided by Christ in such moments. Record that experience in the Family in Faith Journal.

Fun for Review

Prop: Bible

Characters: Person, Good Angel, Evil Angel

Setting: A path or row through the room. EVIL ANGEL stands at one end, GOOD ANGEL at the other.

(PERSON starts down the path toward EVIL ANGEL.)

EVIL ANGEL: Hey, righteous dude! You're on the right path! Keep a comin'! You won't get hurt. This is the way of the day!

GOOD ANGEL: Stop! Wait!

EVIL ANGEL: Butt out, fly-boy! This one's mine!

GOOD ANGEL: Fight the temptation! You're going to get hurt!

PERSON: Well, I know I shouldn't be here.

EVIL ANGEL: Yes, you should! Yes, you should!

GOOD ANGEL: That's right. Say it to the Lord. Talk to Him—He will turn you around. Remember who you are.

PERSON: I'm rotten. That's what I am. I guess this is where I actually belong.

EVIL ANGEL: Bingo!

PERSON: I know I shouldn't be here; but what does it matter? I've done so much to the Lord! Why should He ever forgive someone like me?

EVIL ANGEL: Good question, young lad. Come here, and we'll talk about it.

GOOD ANGEL: Remember who you are. Remember whose name you bear!

EVIL ANGEL: Like he can hear you.

GOOD ANGEL: Or you, for that matter.

EVIL ANGEL: Hey! At least he's on my path! It's in the bag; give it up!

PERSON: *(Falls to his knees to pray)* O Lord, be merciful to me, a sinner! *(Arises and brushes himself off)*

EVIL ANGEL: That's alright! Come on down, let's get touched by an angel. Hey! What's he doing? Where's he going? *(PERSON starts to walk in the opposite direction.)*

GOOD ANGEL: It's called repentance. The Lord changed his heart.

(GOOD ANGEL pushes a Bible in front of PERSON.)

EVIL ANGEL: Hey! You can't do that! That's not fair!

PERSON: *(Picking up the Bible)* Here it is! Thank You, Lord! "For all have sinned and fall short of the glory of God, and are justified freely by His grace through the redemption that came by Christ Jesus" (Romans 3:23–24). And what was my confirmation verse? Oh, yeah, how could I forget? "Be faithful, even to the point of death, and I will give you the crown of life" (Revelation 2:10).

EVIL ANGEL: That's it! I'm outta here! But I'll be back!

GOOD ANGEL: And I'll be waiting.

(EVIL ANGEL exits. GOOD ANGEL exits with PERSON.)

Confession and Absolution

Table Talk

What most shocks you about today's true story?

What kind of slavery does each of us experience?

How do we receive freedom?

Bible Study

Early in His ministry Jesus heals many who are sick. He attracts huge crowds. Read Luke 5:17–26.

1. What might the people have thought was the most immediate need of the paralyzed man?

2. What did Jesus see as the man's most immediate need?

3. In what way are we similar to the paralyzed man?

4. Though the people were impressed with the physical healing of the paralyzed man, what is even more amazing about the spiritual healing that took place?

5. How does Jesus forgive our sins daily?

6. What happens when we acknowledge our sins and confess them before God? before one another?

7. Who in the world or in heaven gives anyone the right to forgive another person? See Matthew 18:18 and John 20:23 if you need help.

8. In what ways might the courts of our land be filled with fewer lawsuits if we practiced the art of confession and absolution more? How might the practice of confession and absolution keep more marriages together?

9. Point out where the Bible story proclaims the Law and the Gospel.

Family in Faith Journal

Complete this sentence: When I admit I've done wrong ... Your parent or mentor should record your comments in the Family in Faith Journal.

Fun for Review

Characters: DJ, Station Manager

Setting: Radio station studio

DJ: *(On air)* Would you like to shed a few extra pounds? Does your midsection need some strengthening? Gotta lotta love in your love handles? If you're looking for a solution to help with your midsection abs, you need to know about Ab Solution. For tighter, firmer abs, you need to get the Ab Solution! This sounds like something I can use, so I'm going to be checking into it this week and letting you know more about it. For more info, try dialing 1-A-B-S-O-L-U-T-I-O-N. Ask for Luke at extension 5-17-26. You're listening to KCIN. And here's the news …

(Takes headphones off and sits back in chair)

STATION MANAGER: *(Entering the studio)* What was that?

DJ: What?

STATION MANAGER: The Ab Solution—for tighter, firmer abs, you need to get Ab Solution!

DJ: I wasn't joking around. I was ab-libbing; I mean *ad*-libbing! I found this note on the console. I thought it was from one of our sponsors, so I put it on the air.

STATION MANAGER: This is a free public-service announcement. It's from the church—my church—down the street. It says that on the back of the paper.

DJ: What's a church doing selling body-building equipment?

STATION MANAGER: They aren't. They asked us to promote a public discussion on Absolution.

DJ: Absolution? You mean one word? It's not 'AB' … 'SOLUTION'? *(Pointing to tummy)*

STATION MANAGER: No.

DJ: So what is Absolution?

STATION MANAGER: It's another word for 'forgiveness.' We confess our sins and receive Absolution—forgiveness. I guess in a way it *is* a body-building power. Confessing our sins and receiving God's forgiveness builds up the body of Christ.

DJ: I'm sorry for messing this up, boss.

STATION MANAGER: You're forgiven!

DJ: My sin has been absolved! Cool!

STATION MANAGER: I guess you weren't so far off. People need to shed a few extra pounds of sin and guilt—Absolution is the way! And Absolution strengthens the body of Christ and our spiritual bodies. And for God to forgive us, He's gotta lotta love through His Son, Jesus!

DJ: I knew it all the time!

STATION MANAGER: The news is almost over.

DJ: But what's up with this Luke guy I told them to ask for?

STATION MANAGER: Luke is a book in the Bible, chapter 5, verses 17–26. That's the story the church is using to discuss the topic. I'll show you when you're off the air.

DJ: Sounds good. The news is over and I'm on! *(Puts headphones on and turns up the volume—is on the air)* Thanks for joining me this afternoon. Before we get back to the music, I have to apologize about the Ab Solution commercial. Here's the real story: You see, it's not about body building …

Table Talk

How might you have reacted if your father or your brother were trapped in the mine?

How did the singing of "A Mighty Fortress" calm the crowd?

Do you have a song or hymn that could comfort you in a similar situation?

Bible Study

After a discussion of greatness in the kingdom of heaven, Jesus turns to the topic of sin, guilt, and forgiveness. Read Matthew 18:10–20.

1. What does Jesus' teaching tell us about the importance of forgiveness? Choose a verse that proves your point.

2. How does it feel when, after you've done something wrong to another person, you ask for forgiveness and the person hugs you or shakes your hand and says, "Of course, I forgive you"? Can you give an example of when this has happened to you?

3. If guilt is defined as "the awareness of having done something wrong" and peace as "inner contentment," why would the reality and consolation of forgiveness bring about peace and freedom from guilt?

4. Though we know we have forgiveness from God, in what way might it be beneficial to receive that forgiveness and consolation privately from a pastor?

5. Point out where the Bible story proclaims the Law and the Gospel.

Family in Faith Journal

With your parent or mentor, consider what you might ask the pastor to help you with. What things wouldn't you ask him to help you with? Record these thoughts in the Family in Faith Journal.

Fun for Review

Prop: Shepherd's rod (just use a yardstick)

Characters: 5 Sheep, Shepherd, someone to make wolf sounds

Setting: A pasture where SHEEP 2-5 are grazing and bleating

SHEEP 2–5: Baaaa! Baaaa! Baaaa! Baaaa!

SHEPHERD: Hello, sheep. What's all the fuss? What's the matter? Let's see now, I need to get a count.

(He looks out into imaginary pasture and uses the rod to count the sheep.)

SHEPHERD: Ninety-six. Ninety-seven. Ninety-eight. Ninety-nine. And … wait a minute! Oh, no! *(SHEEP get restless.)* I had a hundred sheep! Where's the other … ?

(SHEPHERD exits.)

SHEEP 2: Oh, there he goes. Poor master …

SHEEP 3: This makes no sense! It's only ONE sheep. There's ninety-nine of us left!

SHEEP 4: That rotten sheep doesn't even deserve the master's energy.

SHEEP 5: Now, now. He knows what he's doing. Each of us is equally important to the master.

(SHEEP 1 wanders aimlessly and scared. Wolf sounds in the background.)

SHEEP 1: Oh, this is *baaaad*! This was not a very good idea. What was that? I'm so scared. I know I shouldn't have left. I know I shouldn't have said those things to my wooly friends. Oh, I wish I were back in the green pastures near the still water! Oh, I'm lost … what was that? Who's out there?

(SHEEP 1 sits on the floor, curled up, sobbing. SHEPHERD arrives and immediately goes to SHEEP 1. He kneels down and rubs SHEEP 1's back.)

SHEPHERD: Oh, foolish sheep. Why did you leave me? You could have been killed. You were lost, but now you are found. I should put you on my shoulders and carry you home … but you look like you've put on a few pounds. You'll just have to follow me. Let's go! *(SHEEP 1 follows SHEPHERD. Cut back to the pasture.)*

SHEPHERD: Look! My sheep. I have found him!

SHEEP: *(Looking up in amazement)* Baaaa! Baaaa! Baaaa! Baaaa!

(SHEPHERD leaves. He locks the gate.)

SHEEP 2: So how was your great day of independence?

SHEEP 3: Yeah, why did you come *baaaack*?

SHEEP 1: That was a pretty dumb thing to do, fellas. I should never have left.

SHEEP 2: We forgive you.

SHEEP 1: You don't know how glad I am to hear you say that in person! If the master wouldn't have come for me, I would have never found my way back. I was in *saaaad* shape thinking I would never see any of you again—and never get to tell you I was sorry.

SHEEP 5: We're glad you're *baaaaack*! Right, everyone?

ALL SHEEP: *Baaaaack! Baaaack! Baaaack*!

Office of the Keys 32

Table Talk

Is there anything you can do to pay for your own sins and gain peace with God? Explain your answer.

According to St. Paul's letter to the Romans, who declares us righteous and worthy of the kingdom of heaven?

How is the example of Luther encouraging to you?

Bible Study

After an argument with the Pharisees and Saducees, Jesus warns His disciples about the Pharisees' teachings. He then asks His disciples a life-changing question. Read Matthew 16:13–19.

1. According to Jesus (vv. 17–19), what serves as the foundation of the church?

2. What opens the kingdom of heaven?

3. What closes the kingdom of heaven?

4. Who has been given the authority to forgive sins or to withhold forgiveness?

5. At Sunday morning Divine Service, whom has the church "called" to exercise this authority?

6. Share a time in your life when you felt especially joyful and thankful for the forgiveness God offered you.

7. Does everyone who speaks words of confession automatically get forgiven? Who does not receive forgiveness? Why not?

8. Point out how the Bible story proclaims the Law and the Gospel.

Family in Faith Journal

Describe a time when you were locked out (e.g., from your home or a car). Did the experience change the way you did things in the future? Who had the key? How is this like the Office of the Keys? Your parent or mentor should record the story in the Family in Faith Journal.

Fun for Review

Props: Several keys strung together

Characters: Jenny, Marlys, Stu (who has a large collection of keys hanging from his belt loop)

Setting: Anywhere

JENNY: What's up with all the keys, Stu?

MARLYS: You look like the school janitor.

STU: I've started collecting them.

JENNY: Do you have to hang your collection from your pants?

MARLYS: It looks kind of weird.

STU: I think it looks cool.

JENNY: Are you trying to make a fashion statement or something?

STU: No, I just want to be prepared.

MARLYS: For what? Hoping to be named honorary locksmith of the week?

JENNY: Hoping the President of the United States will name you to a *key* cabinet position?

STU: No! It's bigger than that!

JENNY: Let's see, *key*note speaker at the United Nations? Or janitor to the Ambassadors' Club?

MARLYS: I give up.

STU: You guys think you're so smart. You'll see. I'm collecting keys to the kingdom.

JENNY: What kingdom?

STU: The kingdom of God.

MARLYS: You've lost your mind, Stu. Keys for the kingdom of God? You mean … heaven?

STU: Yep.

JENNY: And do you think one of those keys you have is going to get you into heaven?

STU: I'm not sure about that.

MARLYS: What a minute. Does this have to do with the Office of the Keys that Pastor Jon was talking about last week?

STU: That's the one.

JENNY: You're a little mixed up, my friend.

MARLYS: I'll say!

STU: But we were talking about what Peter said when Jesus asked him, "Who do people say that I am?"

JENNY: And Peter said that although the people gave different answers, He knew He was the Christ, the Son of the living God.

STU: Then it says that Jesus gave him the "keys of the kingdom of heaven." When I die, I want to make sure I have the keys to the kingdom.

JENNY: I think the *key* to this conversation is that you are confused, Stu!

MARLYS: The key to the kingdom isn't made of metal or whatever keys are made of.

JENNY: The key to getting into the kingdom of heaven is knowing Jesus in a personal way.

MARLYS: It's about having His forgiveness through Baptism, His Word, and the Lord's Supper.

JENNY: It's about having faith in Jesus.

STU: So having God's forgiveness through Jesus and confessing Him as my Savior opens heaven for me?

JENNY: You've got it!

STU: So without realizing it, I've had the key to heaven all along—ever since the Holy Spirit created faith in me at my Baptism.

MARLYS: I think he's figured it out!

STU: First thing I'm doing is getting rid of all these keys hanging from my belt loop. They were pulling my pants down anyway!

Sacrament of the Altar

Bible Study

The leaders of Judah plot to take Jesus' life. Judas—one of Jesus' disciples—arranges for Jesus' arrest. Knowing all of this, Jesus focuses on having one last meal with the disciples before His death. Read Matthew 26:17-30.

1. What did Jesus know would happen to Him soon? See verse 21.

2. Even with that knowledge, what did Jesus do with the disciples?

3. Contrast Jesus' actions with our own when we've been betrayed or hurt by a friend. Afterward do we want to talk with the friend, much less eat with him or her? In what way is Holy Communion a meal of oneness for us on Sunday morning, despite our differences?

4. What does Jesus announce He's giving through this Supper? See verses 26–28.

5. Read 1 Corinthians 10:16. Besides bread and wine, what else is received according to St. Paul?

6. The Bible in no way suggests that the body and blood are only there symbolically. So why do you think some churches feel compelled to teach only a symbolic presence in the Supper?

7. Explain in your own words why Holy Communion is so important for considering that Jesus comes in, with, and under the bread and wine with His very presence.

8. Recall a special victory celebration, such as after your team has won the area soccer tournament. How is the Lord's Supper an even greater celebration of victory?

9. Point out where the Bible passage proclaims the Law and the Gospel.

Family in Faith Journal

Ask your parent or mentor to explain what it means for him or her to attend Holy Communion. Record the answer in the Family in Faith Journal.

Fun for Review

Props: Bible, notebook paper and pencil, notepad and pen, calculator

Characters: Bobby, Suzy, Amy, Narrator, Billy

Setting: A classroom with a desk or two

(BOBBY is working with a calculator, pencil, and notebook paper.)

SUZY: *(Enters with AMY)* What are you doing?

BOBBY: Excuse me, Sooz, I'm busy.

SUZY: I say, Sir William, this is STUDY HALL! You shouldn't be working so hard.

BOBBY: I'm trying to come up with a formula that proves Christ is truly present in the Lord's Supper. That way Billy can't argue about things like he usually does.

AMY: What?

BOBBY: I think I can prove that Christ's body and blood are truly present in the bread and wine.

AMY: And how long have you been working on this *formula*?

BOBBY: A while. Now, if you don't mind!

SUZY: I have an idea that might help you, little Luther.

BOBBY: *(Perking up)* You do?

SUZY: Sure. Ask the pastor if you can have one of those pieces of bread. Get a microscope from the lab and, get this—look at it!

BOBBY: Hmmmm.

AMY: Both of you—that's ridiculous! That's not how you do it. You don't need a microscope or a calculator, you need a Bible! Have you considered the Bible in your formula, Bobby?

BOBBY: Yeah, but that doesn't actually prove that Christ is really present in this Sacrament. It just says that He is.

AMY: And you have a problem with that?

BOBBY: No, I don't. But what about Billy? He probably thinks it's just an exaggeration or something. If I could just point him to a formula or something that proves it.

(AMY gets a Bible.)

AMY: How about pointing him to this from the Gospel of Matthew: "While they were eating, Jesus took bread, gave thanks and broke it, and gave it to His disciples, saying, 'Take and eat; this is My body.' Then He took the cup, gave thanks and offered it to them, saying, 'Drink from it, all of you. This is My blood.'"

BOBBY: I thought of that. But then Billy will say, "Yeah, but Jesus also says that He is the vine and we are the branches." Then he'll say, "Does that mean every grapevine is actually Jesus?"

AMY: Of course not. Remind him that we interpret God's Word by taking into account the other Scripture passages around it. And nowhere does it say you can sin against a grapevine. But it does say you can sin against the body and blood of Jesus if you take the Lord's Supper in an unworthy manner.

BOBBY: Like not believing that Christ is really present or doubting His Word! See my problem?

NARRATOR: The next morning, before confirmation class …

(BOBBY, AMY, and SUZY approach BILLY, who is about to go into class. He looks suspiciously at the three. They look determined.)

AMY: We have a question or two to ask you, Billy.

BILLY: What?

BOBBY: *(Pulling out a notepad and pen like a detective ready to take notes)* How do you feel about the Lord's Supper?

BILLY: I can't wait for First Communion. And no wisecracks! I'm really looking forward to taking the Lord's Supper. *(Looking at BOBBY's notepad)* What are you doing?

BOBBY: Do you really believe that Jesus is present in the Lord's Supper?

BOBBY: Of course!

AMY and SUZY: YOU DO?

BOBBY: *(A little antagonistic)* How do you know for sure?

BILLY: It's called faith, Bobby-boy!

SUZY: *(Ripping the notepad and pen away from BOBBY and playing detective)* Yeah, but how can you be certain you're not just receiving something that represents the body and blood of Christ?

BILLY: Because Jesus said, "This IS My body" and "This IS My blood." Jesus created the world, was born of a virgin, and rose from the dead. Why should I doubt His Word in the Lord's Supper?

SUZY: There's your formula, Sir Robert. God's promise yields *faith*.

Bible Study

God gives the apostle John visions of the end of the world and the glory of heaven. Read Revelation 19:4–9

1. How does John describe heaven?

2. Who attends this heavenly party?

3. Where do the righteous acts of the saints come from? See verse 8.

4. If in the Lord's Supper we celebrate the real presence of Christ's body and blood, what will we celebrate in heaven someday? See verse 9.

5. Read Matthew 26:29. What promise about heaven does Jesus connect with the Lord's Supper?

6. If worship centers around the Lord's Supper in heaven, what should our worship here on earth center around?

7. If the Lord's Supper is so wonderful, why not fly a plane over all the large cities of the world and simply drop the Lord's Supper in little packets so that everyone receives the blessings?

8. Point out where the passage proclaims the Law and the Gospel.

Family in Faith Journal

Your parent or mentor will describe why he or she goes to Communion. How does your parent or mentor prepare for Communion? Record these thoughts in the Family in Faith Journal.

Fun for Review

Characters: Mrs. Bunt, Shawn

Setting: Bakery

SHAWN: Hi, Mrs. Bunt. I saw your "Help Wanted" sign in the bakery window. I'm here because I need a job.

MRS. BUNT: Hi, Shawn! It's a treat to see you two days in a row—at church yesterday and now you're here for a job. Why do you need a job?

SHAWN: I need some spending money because my parents don't give me enough allowance.

MRS. BUNT: And what do you need to spend this money on?

SHAWN: I need to buy cool clothes. I need money to pay for junk food when I go out with my friends. I need money to spend on stuff when we go on vacation this summer.

MRS. BUNT: Sounds like you are in desperate need, Shawn.

SHAWN: You don't need to tell me that! So what's the job you have open?

MRS. BUNT: I need a kneader.

SHAWN: You need a kneader?

MRS. BUNT: I need someone to come in and knead the dough for the breads we make. To make the bread rise, we add yeast and then someone needs to knead the dough. Then we let it sit for a while before we knead the dough again. The dough needs to be kneaded several times before we bake it.

SHAWN: Well, I need a job and you need a kneader. Can we work something out?

MRS. BUNT: Can you start tomorrow?

SHAWN: Do you need me to knead tomorrow? I have a big paper I need to write for confirmation class.

MRS. BUNT: Well, that's important. I guess I don't *need* for you to start tomorrow. What are you supposed to write about for class?

SHAWN: We're studying the Lord's Supper. My assignment is to write about my need for forgiveness, life, and salvation.

MRS. BUNT: I *know* I need that.

SHAWN: Me too, Mrs. Bunt.

MRS. BUNT: You've been telling me this afternoon about what you need. You said you need a job; you need money for junk and stuff; you need spending money.

SHAWN: And you need a kneader! Soon I'll be a professional kneader!

MRS. BUNT: But I'd say that most of those things you mentioned are things you want, not necessarily *need*. There is a difference.

SHAWN: Good point. Maybe that's what I'll write about—the difference between things we want and things we need.

MRS. BUNT: And we need the Lord's Supper most of all. Unfortunately, not everyone realizes that.

SHAWN: I definitely need God's forgiveness and the gift of life in heaven.

MRS. BUNT: That's for sure.

SHAWN: Mrs. Bunt, I think I'll be able to start work for you tomorrow after all. After talking to you, I think I've just about got this paper written.

MRS. BUNT: That would be great, Shawn. You know why?

SHAWN: Because you need a kneader?

MRS. BUNT: That's right. And now you need to get home. And write that report about what we both really need most!

Table Talk

What teachings of the Bible do "Christian Questions with Their Answers" emphasize?

Why are these important for the Lord's Supper?

In view of these questions, should just anyone receive the Lord's Supper?

Bible Study

The congregation in Corinth is deeply troubled and divided. While instructing them about worship, Paul turns to the topic of the Lord's Supper. He reviews many basic teachings with them that they have studied with him before. Read 1 Corinthians 11:17–34.

1. What kind of objection did St. Paul have with the way the Corinthians partook of Holy Communion? See verses 17–22.

2. What kind of examination does Paul recommend we do before partaking of the Lord's Supper?

3. Why do we have to examine ourselves when we're already Christians?

4. Think back on a past lesson regarding the "real presence" of Christ in the Sacrament. What does the phrase "without recognizing the body of the Lord" mean (v. 29)?

5. What joy comes from knowing that one actually receives His real presence in the Lord's Supper?

6. What does verse 26 suggest regarding the frequency of taking Holy Communion?

7. Point out where the Bible passage proclaims the Law and the Gospel.

Family in Faith Journal

Describe a time you felt unworthy of love or friendship.

Fun for Review

Characters: Usher, Person 1, Person 2, Person 3 (a male), Person 4 (a male), Person 5

Setting: People are in a line, ready to approach the Lord's Table. After each person's thoughts are vocalized, the USHER motions to let the person go forward to the Table. The person exits out of view.

(PERSON 1 is checking a watch.)

PERSON 1: Well, look at the time. Boy, is this service long! Maybe I'll leave right after I take Communion. I don't have time to stick around for more singing and prayers and whatever. Well, looks like it's my turn. *(Starting to walk forward)* Now, let's see, what was I supposed to do? Oh yeah, I need to pick up milk on the way home from church today. *(USHER motions PERSON 1 forward.)*

PERSON 2: Look at these people taking Communion. They don't deserve it! Who's that person? I've never seen her before. She's probably not even Lutheran—probably a guest that didn't see our Communion policy. Poor lady—I hope the pastor passes her over. This is for us, lady! She doesn't even realize what she's taking. Oh, I'd like to talk to her. Hey! How come that usher didn't stop her from going up to Communion? There she goes, eating and drinking to her own condemnation! *(USHER motions PERSON 2 forward.)*

PERSON 3: Thank You, Lord, once again, for this opportunity to be strengthened in my faith toward You. I don't deserve the forgiveness I am ready to receive, but I know it's there because of Your love. I pray that this meal would also strengthen me, first to be a better husband, and from there a better father, and from there a better servant in Your kingdom. Amen. *(USHER motions PERSON 3 forward.)*

PERSON 4: I have so much hate in my heart for what she did to me! Forgive her? You have to be kidding me! Good thing I'm going to get forgiveness. *(Looking around)* In fact, I don't think she's even here this morning. Good! I don't want to even see her face! Of course, in a way I hope she is here. Yeah! Then she can see me standing up here, doing just fine. Lookin' good! That's right. Look at me. I'm okay … you little … *(Mumbles under breath)* *(USHER motions PERSON 4 forward.)*

PERSON 5: It's been a while, Lord. You know, I really shouldn't be taking Communion. I haven't forgotten that I'm actually receiving the true body and blood of Jesus Christ—"in, with, and under the bread and wine." I remember that from my confirmation years. But it's been so long since I've been in church. I've done so much to shame You, Lord. I've brought so much shame on myself. You know, Lord, the pastor visited me and asked me to come back. I said I would, and here I am. But should I be here?